YANKEE
YINGLISH

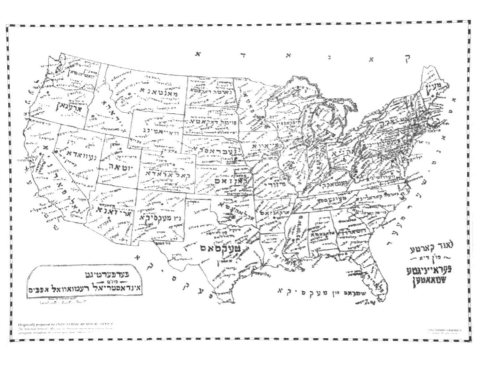

A SOCIOLINGUISTIC STUDY OF YIDDISH ENGLISH
IN NEW YORK'S LOWER EAST SIDE,
FROM THE FIFTIES TO THE PRESENT

RUCHEL JARACH-SZTERN

SECOND EDITION

Acknowledgements

I would like to thank my main Yiddish language informant, Mr. Shayeh Duvid Klapholz, for his precious indications and insights.

I would also like to thank Mrs. Boulot and Mrs. Braquet, my thesis directors and teachers, for their precious advice and guidance.

Notes about the second edition

This work was first presented in September 2009 as a thesis to obtain my Master's Degree in English Language, Literature and Civilization at the University of Marne-la-Vallée, France.

With the intention of making it more accessible, the text has been revised and edited for printing and online diffusion in October 2017.

The present revised text is published as the second edition.

Table of Contents

Introduction

Why Yankee Yinglish?

This book is about the encounter of different cultures, the Yiddish coming from the Old World who met the English of present days in America. The title, Yankee Yinglish, has been chosen to reflect that diversity:

Yinglish is the contration of Yiddish and English, while Yankee, in its broadest sense, symbolizes the United States.

Presentation of the Topic and Issues Involved

The presence of Yiddish in today's American English is noticeable when listening to people talking, watching television, reading advertisements or articles in the press, surfing on the internet, be it on press websites, on private websites or chats and forums. To Yiddish mother tongue speakers, such a presence is immediately noticed by a degree of familiarity with words, phrases not pertaining to common American English. On the contrary, there is to English mother tongue speakers a similar degree of unfamiliarity when coming across the same words, phrases, and feeling that they are not "real" English, while not being able to retrace them to their origin in Yiddish.

In this work we will try to analyze the phenomenon of Yiddish features in American English by dealing with three main issues:

- the issue of diachronic approach to the presence of Yiddish in American English, and of the evolution which may have occurred from the second half of the twentieth century on. In order to analyze this issue we have gathered a corpus which spreads over a time span of some sixty years (from the 1950's to 2009).

- to what extent, and in which domains, the presence of Yiddish is felt in American English today.

- the issue of sociological determiners: to what extent the sex, age, parental origin, occupation, level of religious practice, religious or community affiliation, affect, in quantity or in quality, the use of Yiddish features in American English.

Hypotheses

We formulate a number of working hypotheses regarding these issues:

- Just as Yiddish, *per se* a mixed language, mixed with other languages as easily as it adopted foreign words when meeting other cultures and languages over the course of history, so it has merged with American English. We intend to show that this same plasticity that occurred in the past is found again in today's use of American English.

- We will also try and determine whether there is an evolution from a layer of the corpus to another; and what are the characteristics of this evolution. In this particular context, we formulate the hypothesis that as times goes, and assimilation becomes deeper, the traces of Yiddish fade - except for an amount of untranslatable words and concepts referring to specific objects, practices or ways of thinking, or for very pregnant idiomatic morphological or syntactic features deeply embedded in the Yiddish language, which are therefore transferred into English by Yiddish mother tongue speakers, and finally enter the realm of common American English;

• at the same time, we do not dismiss the possibility that there could be backtrackings in this evolution, that is to say, that we may find periods (or specific themes) for which searching for one's roots would express itself by a return to the ancestral language and thus leave traces on one's practice of American English.

• We expect to find that the level of presence of Yiddish elements in American English is linked to a speaker's level of religious practice, attachment to Jewish identity, and/ or link to a Jewish community. When available, the information about sex, age, parental origin, level of religious practice, religious or community affiliation will thus be attached to the quotations and will allow us to link the examples to the sociolinguistic characteristics of the speakers.

Presentation of the Various Chapters

In **Part One**, we will define Yiddish as a contact and fusion language, that is to say a language which is already in itself a mix of a variety of cultures and civilizations probably unique in its fabric, due to the historical wandering conditions of its speakers throughout time. For the purpose of this presentation we will focus on the basic vocabulary of the Yiddish lexicon as a mirror of the changing history and geography of the Jewish people.

To illustrate the phenomenon of the mixing of languages with Yiddish, we will also analyze an early piece of Yiddish work: Glikel of Hameln's Memoires, written from 1691 to 1719, which provide an early insight into the fabric of Yiddish. Glikel of Hameln was born in 1646 in Hamburg, Germany, and died in 1724 in Metz, France. Her diary deals with her everyday life as a Jewish mother and also as a businesswoman traveling throughout Europe, and contains striking examples of language melting. In this sub-part, we will show a degree of interpenetration of Yiddish and French, and Yiddish and German, as explained by the historical and geographical context of Glikel's life. Glikel traveled a lot, especially between France and Germany, she was in contact with Jews as well as non-Jews, and she adapted each time her vocabulary, consciously or not.

In **Part Two**, we will outline the global historical context of Jewish immigration to America, which started in the 18th century and developed over more than two centuries. We will focus on the historical period of the *en masse* Jewish immigration from the years 1881-1882 onwards. These waves of immigrants were mostly caused by the pogroms that started in Russia and Ukraine and then spred to North-Eastern Europe.

We will then tackle researches about Yiddish and American English, and we will situate our research in this timeline.

In **Part Three** we analyze in depth the presence of Yiddish features in American English and the evolution which has taken place over the course of some sixty years. To this end we have determined four periods and sources.

The collected corpus is the following (for a more complete description of the texts see below, "Presentation of the covered sources and brief historical context"):

- Sign shops in the Lower East Side, dating from the fifties and sixties;

- *A Bintel Brief* (foreword, introduction and English translation), dated 1971.This book is a selection of letters addressed to *The Forward* between 1906 and 1967;

- articles from *The Forward* in English, dated 2003-2009. *The Forward*, founded in 1897, is the main Jewish newspaper in New York, and played an important role as a tool for integration for Jewish immigrants;

- extracts from American Jewish websites, forums, chats, dated 2008-2009, granting us a scope of some sixty years of Yiddish presence in American English.

For each source we first describe its historical context. We then proceed to the in-depth analysis of the linguistic evidence of the mix between Yiddish and American English. For the sake of clarity we stick to the classical categorization of linguistic phenomena into lexicon (presence of Yiddish words and impacted lexical fields), morphological features (English words modified by Yiddish morphological features), and syntactic features (transposition of Yiddish syntax when using English).

For the second period and source (the letters translated from *A Bintel Brief*), we analyze the persistence of Yiddish terms and phrases in the English translation (for a justification of this see below, "Presentation of the covered sources and brief historical context").

In **Part Four**, we interpret the results of the in-depth analysis performed in Part Three under two main aspects:

- the diachronic aspect: has there been an evolution of Yiddish presence in American English over the sixty years covered by our data; if so, is the presence of Yiddish features fading or on the contrary, becoming stronger? is the evolution linear? does it affect the lexical, the morphological or the syntactic features? is there an evolution in the impacted lexical fields?

- the sociological determiners; what is notable in the sociological distribution of the use of morphological, lexical and syntactic features of Yiddish in American English; we will synthesize here the items of information available needed to characterize the discourse: sex, age, occupation, parental origin, level of religious practice, religious or community affiliation, … and try to find correlations between the linguistic features observed and the sociological characteristics of the population studied.

In the **Conclusion**, we will confront the results of this analysis to our working hypotheses about the different issues concerned, in order to determine their validity, or otherwise to refine or amend them.

Presentation of the Covered Sources and Brief Historical Context

Our corpus is made up of the following documents.

First Period and Source: the Years 1950-1960. Signs from Lower East Side Jewish Shops in New York.

Photographs of seven shops presenting religious articles and food, dating from the fifties, situated on Essex Street and on East Houston Street in the Lower East Side.

These documents are either shop signs or writings on the windows of the shops.

For one document we have two photographs available, corresponding to two different periods, the first one taken before 1960, and the second one in the years 2000. A comparative analysis will thus be possible for this document.

Second Period and Source: the 1970's. *A Bintel Brief. Sixty Years of Letters from the Lower East Side to the Jewish Daily Forward.* **Introduction and translation** by Isaac Metzker, **foreword** by Harry Golden.

The book presents the translation of letters of Jewish immigrants written from 1906 to 1967, in Yiddish, to the

Yiddish daily *The Forward* ("Forverts" in Yiddish). *A Bintel Brief* (meaning "A bundle of letters" in Yiddish) was the advice column of *The Forward*, initiated by the *Forward*'s founding editor, Abraham Cahan, in 1906.

Regarding the authors, Isaac Metzker, a long-time editor of *The Forward*, was born in 1900 in Galicia, Poland, and arrived in the United States of America in 1924. Harry Golden was born in Galicia, Poland in 1902. He arrived to New York City in 1905.

The introduction and foreword to the book provide us with a direct insight into an English text dating from the 1970's, mixed with many Yiddish words and phrases. It is in itself a corpus to be investigated.

As for the translation of the letters, we believe that we can analyze this source in the following way: by examining which Yiddish terms were translated into English by Isaac Metzker, and which ones remained untranslated, we can determine which Yiddish words were understandable by the reader of such a book in the years 1970.

Third Period and Source: the Years 2003-2009. *The Forward' Articles* in English.[1]

The Forward is more than a plain newspaper; it has served as a tool for the integration of Jewish immigrants in the Lower East Side since its creation back in 1897: "The *Forverts* [*"Forward"* in Yiddish] helped generations of newcomers adjust to life in America [...] *The Jewish Daily Forward*

---

[1]   Only the years 2003-2009 are available on the internet.

sponsored English classes [...] and a pro-labor summer camp, and hosted vaccination days in the lobby of its building"[2].

Part of the *Forward*'s mission, as pursued by Abraham Cahan, was to help Jews assimilate into American Society, be it at the cost of losing their Yiddish and shifting to English[3].

As presented on the newspaper's website, the *Forward* was launched as a Yiddish-language daily newspaper on April 22, 1897 [...] as a defender of trade unionism and moderate, democratic socialism. *The Jewish Daily Forward* [...] fought for social justice, helped generations of immigrants to enter American life [...] and was among the nation's most eloquent defenders of democracy and Jewish rights. [...] By the early 1930s the Forward had become one of America's premier metropolitan dailies, with a nationwide circulation topping 275,000 [...] At the helm, guiding the paper for a full half-century until his death in 1950, was Cahan. Both as an editor and in his own writings - including his timeless advice column, the Bintel Brief - he set the populist, down-to-earth tone that was the Forward's hallmark. In thousands of Jewish households across the country, the Forward was for decades more than just a daily newspaper - it was a trusted guide and a member of the family[4].

---

[2]   Jennifer Siegel. "*A Community of Readers*", The Forward, (Issue April 6, 2007), http://www.forward.com/articles/10463/

[3]   Gal Beckerman. "Forward Thinking. So what if the Goyim are looking? A Jewish Newspaper lets it all hang out", Columbia University, *Graduate School of Journalism*, Volume 42, Issue 5 (January 2004): 33

[4]   History of *The Forward* on http://forward.com/about/history/

The *Forward*'s founder, Abraham Cahan, was "an assimilationist who believed that immigrants needed to become part of the mainstream of society in their new home [...] He sought to Americanize them", and regularly emphasized "the importance of learning English"[5].

The newspaper had indeed a special feature, *a Bintel Brief,* which has been deemed the first reader's advice column, initiated by the *Forward*'s founding editor, Abraham Cahan, in 1906. The very purpose of this column was to help the new immigrant fit into the American way of life.

The Forward has been published in English since 1987, and it still does reflect an amount of Yiddish features. The articles where these features are mostly to be found are the ones dealing with community, family, food, culture ("Community News, "Art and Culture", "The Schmooze"- itself a Yiddish word in origin[6]-, "Bintel Blog" ...) ; but this trend is subject to exceptions since Yiddish features are also to be found in articles on general politics ("National News", "International News",...).

5   Howard Muggamin, *The Jewish Americans* (New York- Philadelphia: Chelsea House Publishers, 2001): 75
6   From Yiddish "shmou'es", "rumors", taken from Hebrew "shmouot", same meaning.

Fourth Period and Source: the Years 2008-2009.
American Jewish Websites, Forums and Chats.

This collection covers the main American Jewish websites, forums, and chats. As such it encompasses the various tendencies represented in the Jewish community, from the totally secular to the ultra-Orthodox. The contributors' age ranges from 20 to 50.

In the specific case of the forums, from which many examples are taken, they contain informal discussions and the topics are not permanent. They can be edited or deleted by moderators. One forum is sex-segregated and also marital status oriented, as it is strictly reserved to married Orthodox Jewish women. Other forums are geared specifically towards traditional and Orthodox Jews. Some websites are clearly related to a still more specific kind of religious practice *inside* the Orthodox world (Chabad Lubavitch Chasidim, Yeshivish). One forum is meant for all Jews. The participants range from totally secular to Orthodox. Some websites do clearly carry a pedagogical orientation, implying that they are oriented towards totally secular Jews, or to non-Jews willing to learn about Judaism.

Each quotation will be referred to its website/ forum of origin and, when available, to its author's sociological affiliation.

As an Appendix, we present a Glossary of Yiddish terms.

Concerning the general accuracy of the meaning of Yiddish terms and citations in this work, we have relied on Shayeh Duvid Klapholz. He was born in 1925 in Krakow, Poland (Galicia), from a Chasidish Jewish family. An oral tradition has it that the Klapholz family came to Krakow from Frankfort-on-Mein. Shayeh Duvid Klapholz is of Yiddish mother tongue. As a child and an adolescent, he attended a Jewish school (Yesodei Hatorah, "the basis of the Torah"). The morning was devoted to general studies (teaching language was Polish) and the afternoon was devoted to religious studies (teaching language was Yiddish). A UN refugee in April 1945 after being liberated from Bergen Belsen concentration camp, he has always kept very strong links to the Yiddish language and culture, and lives now in Israel.

Part One:
Overview of Yiddish

I. Yiddish as a "Contact" and a "Fusion" Language

The authoritative YIVO[7] provides us with the following description of the origin of Yiddish language:

> The most accepted [...] theory of the origin of Yiddish is that it began to take shape by the 10th century as Jews from France and Italy migrated to the German Rhine Valley. They developed a language that included elements of Hebrew, Jewish-French, Jewish-Italian, and various German dialects. In the late Middle-Ages, when Jews settled in Eastern Europe, Slavic elements were incorporated into Yiddish[8].

Although "there is controversy concerning whether the development of the Yiddish language as a whole should be viewed in terms of monogenesis from Middle High German, or polygenesis from a set of source languages"[9], the two positions need not be contradictory. However, the development of Yiddish cannot be described as a creolization: first, this phenomenon is not defined by linguistic criteria only, but also by sociological ones like the domination of a civilization over another, more "primitive" one (the German culture did not dominate the Jewish one); and secondly, in the

---

[7]   The YIVO (Institute for Jewish Research) in New York, founded as the Jewish Scientific Institute in Vilna, Poland in 1925, is an acknowledged authority on the Yiddish language.
[8]   YIVO website, http://www.yivoinstitute.org/yiddish/alefbeys_fr.htm
[9] Adam Albright, "Base-driven leveling in Yiddish verb paradigms" (MIT Draft: November 2006) 1. http://web.mit.edu/albright/www/papers/Albright-LevelingInYiddishVerbs.pdf

process of creolization we witness a simplification of the adopted dominant language : Yiddish as a language has a history; it cannot be defined as a "simplification" of Middle High German, but rather as an evolution thereof, much like the evolution having taken place from Middle High German to Standard German:

> Modern Yiddish is clearly descended from Old Yiddish, a highly inflected sister language of Middle High German. In fact, the line between 'Judeo-German', i.e. Middle High German with a 'Jewish accent', and Old Yiddish, a separate language from Middle High German, is often not clear.[10].

The derivation of Yiddish grammar from German can be traced back to Middle High German (*Mittel Hoch Deutsch*, a period going from the12th century to the beginning of the 16th), as is the case for example for Yiddish's "verbal inflectional morphology, which can be traced back almost exclusively to a German source"[11].

The vocabulary is also a witness of this early derivation. This is attested by the presence in today's Yiddish of German words which go back to Middle High German, and which no longer belong to the German lexicon of today, as with:

[10]   Ellen F. Prince, *Yiddish as a Contact Language*, in « Creolization and Contact », Creole Language Library Volume 23, edited by Norval Smith and Tonjes Veenstra (University of Amsterdam-Free University Berlin, 2001, vi, 323 pp.): 263

[11]   Adam Albright, "Base-driven leveling in Yiddish verb paradigms" (MIT Draft: November 2006): 1 http://web.mit.edu/albright/www/papers/Albright-LevelingInYiddishVerbs.pdf

Yiddish *"farfl"*, "crumb of dough", from Middle High German "verveln", same meaning[12]

Yiddish *"enk"*, "you", from Middle High German "ënk", "you"[13].

Yiddish *"breileft"*[14], "wedding", from Middle High German "Brautlauf"[15]; "Broutlouf"or "Bruon- [bride] loff [run], was a word used to designate the marriage in South-Western Germany in reference to a custom where the winner of a race was chosen as the groom.[16].

Others German words present from Middle High German to today found their place in the Yiddish lexicon:

"Zun", "son", from "Sohn". "sunu". The Middle High German word is "sunu"

"Sheyn", "beautiful", from "schön". The Middle High German word is "sconi"

"Mentsch", "decent person, man", from "Mensch", "human". The word has not changed from Middle High German.

"Groys", "big", from "gross". The Middle High German word is "groz"

[12]   Alexander Harkavy, *Yiddish-English-Hebrew Dictionary* (New York: Hebrew Publishing Company, 1928): 397. The dictionary also deals with etymology.
[13]   Alexander Harkavy, *Yiddish-English-Hebrew Dictionary* (New York: Hebrew Publishing Company, 1928): 351
[14]   "Breileft" is ancient and is no more used in today's Yiddish. The word "khasseneh" (from Hebrew "khatunah", "wedding"), is used instead. Personal communication from our informant Shayeh Duvid Klapholz.
[15]   Alexander Harkavy, *Yiddish-English-Hebrew Dictionary* (New York: Hebrew Publishing Company, 1928): 134
[16]   « Wette, wedding. Un texte inconnu de Mauss », in Revue française de sociologie année 1985, Volume 26, n° 26-2 : 263
http://www.persee.fr/web/revues/home/prescript/article/rfsoc_0035-2969_1985_num_26_2_3948

"Tochte", "daughter", from "Tochter". The Middle High German word is "tohter"[17]

Although "Yiddish became a language of its own sometime between 900 and 1100 CE", it is difficult to be more precise as "in its early days, Yiddish was primarily a spoken language rather than a written language"[18]. Eventually Yiddish became also a written language, the first traces of it dating back to the thirteenth and fourteenth centuries[19].

Most of the time, Yiddish is written in the Hebrew alphabet, but for reading convenience we will transcribe it in Latin characters.

The document on the next page retraces the Jews' presence in Europe at the time of the emergence of Yiddish as a language of its own.

---

[17] All these references are from Max Weinreich, *History of the Yiddish Language* (Originally published in 1973 in Yiddish by the YIVO Institute for Jewish Research). With Paul Glasser, Shlomo Noble (translation): *History of the Yiddish Language* (London- New Haven: Yale University Press, Yale Language Series, 2008): 604-658

[18] Tracey R Rich on www.Jewfaq.org/yiddish.htm

[19] Chava Turniansky, *Les langues juives dans le monde ashkénaze traditionnel*, in Baumgarten Jean, Ertel Rachel, et al. : *Mille ans de cultures ashkénazes* (Paris : Liana Lévi, 1994): 422

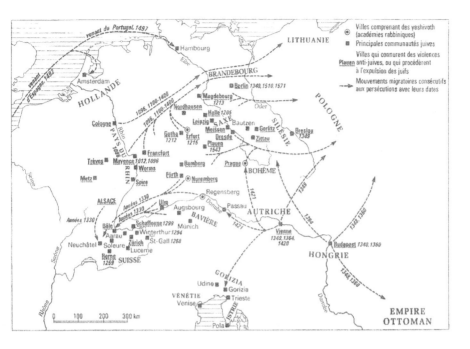

Image 1: Jews of Central Europe, 1000-1500, and their migrations. [20]

The map shows that the bulk of Jewish presence was then situated on a territory that corresponds to East of France and Germany of today or, to be more precise:

> En Allemagne, séparée de l'Empire franc dès 843 (traité de Verdun), les communautés juives les plus anciennes se situent en Lorraine, en Franconie, en Souabe, et le long des rives du Rhin ; plus tard, elles s'infiltrèrent sur le cours supérieur du Danube et de l'Elbe et pénétrèrent en Bavière, en Autriche, en Bohême[21].

[20]   Rachel Ertel, *Le Shtetl. La bourgade juive de Pologne* (Paris : Payot, 1982) :
26
[21]   André Chouraqui, *Histoire du judaïsme* (Paris : P.U.F., 1968): 80

As the map clearly shows, very important cultural and religious centers, gathered around rabbinic academies, were established in this region:

> Talmudic learning, which had established a principal stronghold in the Rhineland, was enriched by an illustrious line of scholars and religious leaders, such as [...] the rabbinic Kalonymus family of Mainz, Rabbi Meir of Rothenburg [...] the Jews were by no means impervious to outside cultural influences [...] Jews spoke German, even if they wrote it with Hebrew characters and employed Hebrew phonetics instead of German. By adding Hebrew words and expressions to German, in time they created a distinctive language-Yiddish[22].

As mentioned previously, "La formation de la langue Yiddish comme langue de contact et de fusion montre à l'évidence l'interpénétration des deux sociétés"[23]; a direct consequence of this interpenetration was that Yiddish evolved as mainly a mix of German and Hebrew. Although a number of other languages did affect Yiddish, due to the Jews' wanderings in the course of centuries, as previously said the sociological context of the evolution of Yiddish excludes this language from the group of creoles.

---

[22]   Nathan Ausubel, *Pictorial History of the Jewish People* (New York, Crown Publishers, 1962): 122
[23]   Rachel Ertel, *Le Shtetl. La bourgade juive de Pologne* (Paris : Payot, 1982): 18

It will be trivial to say that an important part of the Yiddish lexicon (estimated as high as 20 % of it)[24] can be traced back to Hebrew; as these examples show:

"Almone", "widow", from Hebrew "almana" (same meaning)[25]

"Yontef", "holiday", from Hebrew "Yom tov" ("good day")[26]

"Sukko", "cabin", from Hebrew "sukka"[27] (same meaning, in reference to a location in the Desert of Sinai where the Hebrew people rested and build cabins after fleeing from Egypt)·

"Chaye", "alive, living", from Hebrew "chay" (same meaning)[28]

Moreover, a situation of diglossia/ triglossia clearly characterized Jewish linguistic usages in history; it can be described as:

> la présence simultanée, avec le Yiddish, du *loshn koydesh* (langue sacrée) et d'au moins une langue coterritoriale non juive [...] de façon diglossique/ triglossique typique, tous ces langages étaient

---

[24] Ellen F. Prince, *Yiddish as a Contact Language*, in « Creolization and Contact », Creole Language Library Volume 23, edited by Norval Smith and Tonjes Veenstra (University of Amsterdam-Free University Berlin, 2001, vi, 323 pp.): 264

[25] Max Weinreich, *History of the Yiddish Language* (Originally published in 1973 in Yiddish by the YIVO Institute for Jewish Research). With Paul Glasser, Shlomo Noble (translation): *History of the Yiddish Language* (London- New Haven: Yale University Press, Yale Language Series, 2008): 604-658

[26] Alexander Harkavy, *Yiddish-English-Hebrew Dictionary* (New York, Hebrew Publishing Company 1928): 385

[27] Max Weinreich, Paul Glasser, Shlomo Noble (translation). *History of the Yiddish Language, Volumes 1 and 2*. (London- New Haven: Yale University Press, Yale Language Series, 2008): 604-658. Unless otherwise stated, the following examples of lexical borrowings of Yiddish from other languages will be taken from this source.

[28] "THE GIVEN NAMES DATA BASES" (GNDBs) Professor G. L. Esterson, Ra'anana, Israel.

> fonctionnellement légitimés par la communauté elle-
> même [...] la connaissance de ces langues répondait aux
> besoins de la communauté, sur le plan interne aussi bien
> que sur le plan externe[29].

Wherever they may have settled, the Jews always learned Old Hebrew (named "Loshn Koydesh", "holy language") for religious purposes, and also learned the local language, this leading to a systematic diglossia (usage of a common, vernacular language and an ancient, traditional one as second language). When a new structured, independent contact language emerged, as in Eastern Europe with Yiddish, a situation of triglossia was generalized. From the tenth to the nineteenth century, Yiddish was the vernacular language, Loshn Koydesh the traditional one and the local language (German, Polish, Russian...) was used to communicate with non-Jewish people.

So important has been the fusion between German and Hebrew words in the Yiddish lexicon, that one can also find Hebrew and German words mixed in one single expression:

"Shayne kalloh", "beautiful bride", from Middle High German "sconi" and Hebrew "kallah".

"Kineine hore", "without evil eye", from Middle High German "nihein" and Hebrew "ayn ha ra", "evil eye".

"Vilde Chayye", "wild beast", from Middle High German "wild" and Hebrew "chayya" ("beast").

---

[29]   Yoshua Fishman, *"Sociologie du yiddish"*, dans A. Baumgarten, R. Ertel et al., Mille ans: 428

Let alone phrases, some Yiddish *words* are in themselves a result of the two languages' mixing. And this is still more impressive. May be, there comes a time when the intensity of "contact" between two languages may amount to "fusion". It seems to us that this moment is reached when one word (usually a unity, an entity), comes to be constituted of two very clearly distinctive roots, a Semitic one and a Germanic one for instance, like in these examples:

"kvatter", which is the combination of Hebrew "kavod", "honor", and Middle High German "turi"[30], "door". It means the person who brings the baby "through the door", in the synagogue, to be circumcised;

The well-known Yiddish word "shlimazl", which is the combination of Middle High German word "slim", "crooked", and Hebrew "mazal", "destiny". It means someone who is always unlucky.

"Tehilimsager", from Hebrew "Tehilim", King David's book of Psalms and Middle High German "sagen", to say. It designates a person whose occupation is saying psalms in memory of dead people. According to the Jewish custom, saying psalms after someone's death helps the person's soul entering the Garden of Eden (Heaven).

---

[30]   Max Weinreich, *History of the Yiddish Language* (Originally published in 1973 in Yiddish by the YIVO Institute for Jewish Research). With Paul Glasser, Shlomo Noble (translation): *History of the Yiddish Language* (London- New Haven: Yale University Press, Yale Language Series, 2008): 604-658

In this sense Yiddish is indeed and essentially a "contact language"[31], derived from Middle High German, with at the beginning mostly borrowings from Hebrew, and with a generally "massive lexical borrowing"[32] trend having manifested itself in the course of history and touching a dozen of languages.

Hebrew and German forming obviously the basis and main components of Yiddish, we will now briefly present some examples in order to illustrate the variety of other historical borrowings of Yiddish from other European (and non-European) languages.

We find in Yiddish, through Hebrew, traces of languages of the Antiquity: Aramaic, Greek, Latin. These are testimonials to the encounter of the Hebrew language with these cultures and languages, be it by the deportation of the Hebrew people in the territory of Persia / Babylonia (whose language was Aramaic), in the sixth century BC (586), or by the conquest of the Land of Israel by the Greek and Roman armies, from the fourth century BC to the second century CE.

A good example of this will be the Hebrew term « apikoros », directly derived from the Greek philosopher's name Epicure ("epikouros"), which came to mean "heretic" in Mishnaic Hebrew[33], as we see in a passage of *Pirké Abot*[34], a religious

---

[31]   Ellen F. Prince, *Yiddish as a Contact Language*, in « Creolization and Contact », Creole Language Library Volume 23, edited by Norval Smith and Tonjes Veenstra (University of Amsterdam-Free University Berlin, 2001, vi, 323 pp.): 263

[32]   Ellen F. Prince: 264

[33]   Mireille Hadas-Lebel, *Histoire de la langue hébraïque des origines à l'époque de la Mishna*. (Paris: Publications Orientalistes de France, 1977): 146

[34]   Pirké Aboth. *Traité des principes ou recueil de préceptes et de sentences des pères de la synagogue* (Paris : librairie Durlacher, 1957) : 8

writing from the second century AD[35]: "Know what to answer an *Apikoros*"[36]. Perceived as putting pleasure over everything, the epicurean philosophy was in every point opposed to the Jewish traditional teaching who emphasizes duty. Epicure's name was therefore attached to almost every belief opposed to the Jewish values, especially heretic ones. Much later, this word entered (through Hebrew) into Yiddish, the meaning of "epikoïres" in Yiddish[37] being "heretic".

For the purpose of this outline we present a few more examples to further illustrate the melting of other ancient languages into Hebrew and then into Yiddish:

From Aramaic: "segula", we have Yiddish "segule", "treasure, amulet", "a treasured possession"

From Greek: "phoibos", "bright" we have Yiddish "Feibush"[38] (a male name, which is also used for a handsome man, probably because Phoibos was an epithet of the Greek god Apollo)

From Greek: "margarites", we have Yiddish "Margolis", "pearl"[39]

---

[35] Eric Smilévitch, Introduction aux Commentaires du traité des Pères (*Pirké Avot*), (Lagrasse, Editions Verdier 1990) : 12

[36] Pirke Avoth, Chapter II, 14

[37] Uriel Weinreich, Modern English-Yiddish, Yiddish-English Dictionary (New York: YIVO institute for Jewish Research – McGraw-Hill Book Company, 1968)

[38] Max Weinreich, *History of the Yiddish Language* (Originally published in 1973 in Yiddish by the YIVO Institute for Jewish Research). With Paul Glasser, Shlomo Noble (translation): *History of the Yiddish Language* (London- New Haven: Yale University Press, Yale Language Series, 2008): 604-658

[39] "THE GIVEN NAMES DATA BASES" (GNDBs) Professor G. L. Esterson, Ra'anana, Israel

<u>From Greek:</u> "kalonymos", "beautiful name", we have "Klonimus" (a male name)[40]

<u>From Latin:</u> "Drusilla" (a female name), we have "Dreisel" (a Yiddish female name)

<u>From Latin:</u> "vitalis", "related to life", we have Yiddish "Faytl"

<u>From Latin:</u> "dulcis", "sweet", we have Yiddish "Toltse"[41].

Interestingly enough, these ancient layers seem to have produced quite a few Yiddish first names, a witness of the Jews' will of cultural integration into the concerned cultures, as the choice of one's child's name is (to this day) an affective, identity related, and engaging issue.

In addition to these ancient layers, and starting from the dispersion of the Hebrew people throughout Europe after the Second Temple's destruction in 70 CE[42], the wanderings of Jews in Europe in the course of centuries eventually resulted in the mixing of various European languages into the Yiddish lexicon: French, Spanish, Italian, Slavic languages, as well as Turkish, ... And thus we find, in Yiddish, borrowings such as these:

<u>from French:</u>

"Bunem", "good man", from "bon homme"

---

[40] "THE GIVEN NAMES DATA BASES" (GNDBs) Professor G. L. Esterson, Ra'anana, Israel

[41] For the three examples above, the reference is Max Weinreich, *History of the Yiddish Language* (Originally published in 1973 in Yiddish by the YIVO Institute for Jewish Research). With Paul Glasser, Shlomo Noble (translation): *History of the Yiddish Language* (London- New Haven: Yale University Press, Yale Language Series, 2008): 604-658

[42] Ygaël Yadin, Ygael. *Bar-Kokhba, The Rediscovery of the Legendary Hero of the Last Jewish Revolt Against Imperial Rome* London - Jerusalem : Weidenfeld & Nicholson and Steimatsky, 1971)

"Bentschen", "to bless, to pray", from "bénir"

"Shneyer", "lord", from "seigneur"

"Mushkat", "muscat", from "muscat"

"Kneidel", "matzo ball" (matza that comes in contact with water[43]), from "quenelle"

"Tscholent", a kind of food served on holidays, from "chaud-lent"[44]

"Yachet", "hyacinth", from "hyacinthe"[45]

It is interesting here to note the semantic fields involved in the borrowings: "nature", especially food.

from Spanish:

"Krasa", "grace", from "gracia"

from Italian:

"Vite", "life", from "vita"

"Beyle", "beautiful", from "bella"

"Bendet", "blessed", from "benedetto"

"Yent, yenta", "noble", from "gente"

From Slavic Languages:

"Dobrisch", "good", from "dobre"[46]

---

[43] http://halachicinsights.blogspot.com/2009/04/more-pesach-insights.html

[44] The five above examples are from Max Weinreich, *History of the Yiddish Language* (Originally published in 1973 in Yiddish by the YIVO Institute for Jewish Research). With Paul Glasser, Shlomo Noble (translation): *History of the Yiddish Language* (London- New Haven: Yale University Press, Yale Language Series, 2008): 604-658

[45] THE GIVEN NAMES DATA BASES (GNDBs) Professor G. L. Esterson, Ra'anana, Israel

[46] The five last examples are from Max Weinreich, *History of the Yiddish Language* (Originally published in 1973 in Yiddish by the YIVO Institute for Jewish Research). With Paul Glasser, Shlomo Noble (translation): *History of the Yiddish Language* (London- New Haven: Yale University Press, Yale Language Series, 2008): 604-658

"Badan", "God-given", from "bogdan"[47]

From Turkish:

"Yarmulke", "kippa", from Turk. "yaghmurluk", a sort of cap[48]

"Prakes", "stuffed cabbage", from Turk. "yaprak", "leaf"[49]

These brief examples show that the Yiddish lexicon is in itself the mirror of a mosaic of languages, a mixing of a variety of cultures and civilizations probably unique in its fabric, due to the historical conditions of wandering of its speakers throughout time and territories.

II. An Early Illustration of the Mixing of Languages in Yiddish : 18th Century's Glikel of Hameln's Memoires

In order to further show this phenomenon of mixing of languages in Yiddish we will analyze Glikel of Hameln's *Memoires,* which provides an early insight into the fabrics of Yiddish. Written from 1691 to 1719, it is typical of Western Yiddish in the 1600's. Glikel of Hameln was born in 1646 in Hamburg, Germany, and died in 1724 in Metz, France. Her diary deals with her everyday life as a Jewish mother of fourteen and businesswoman traveling throughout Europe, and contains striking examples of language melting.

---

[47]   THE GIVEN NAMES DATA BASES (GNDBs) Professor G. L. Esterson, Ra'anana, Israel,

[48]   Merriam Webster Online Dictionary

[49]   *The Forward*, published July 24, 2008, issue of August 01, 2008: 4.

On page 130, we encounter the phrase "viel gedoktiert", someone who has "run from doctor to doctor". It is from German "viel", "a lot", and Latin "doctor".

On page 142, ref. 6, we find "kredit ktav", a letter of credit, from French "crédit", "credit" and Hebrew "ktav", meaning "writing, letter".

On page 266, ref. 104, we find "mit ein grosse svit", "with a big escort", the three first words being Yiddish, and the last one French, from "suite", "escort".

On page 294, ref. 301, we find "baali zich ekskuzirt", "my husband apologized". The first word is Hebrew ("baal" means "husband", and the final "I" is a possessive mark), the second word is from German ("sich", the German reflexive form), and the third one is from French, with a Latin origin "s'excuser", "to apologize").

On page 294 again, ref. 305, "den ist be emes ein printsipal shiduch gevesen", "it was really a top class wedding". "Den ist [...] gevesen" and "ein" are German, meaning "it has been" and "a", "be emes" comes from Hebrew "be emet", "in truth". "Printsipal" comes from French (Latin origin) "principal", "important, top class".

On page 318, ref. 452, we find the word "miserabil", from French "misérable", "miserable".

Although this can seem surprising, this type of bi-lingual words are also to be found in Ladino, the Sephardic (Spanish) equivalent of Yiddish, which is a mix of Spanish, Hebrew and the languages mentioned for Yiddish. For example, the Ladino female name "Adizbuena" is said to come from Turkish "ediz", "highly", and Spanish "buena", "good". Another one,

"Orocidi", comes from Spanish "oro", "gold", and Turkish "çidi", "lady". "Fazbuena", another first name, from Arabic "faiz", "victory" and Spanish "buena", "good".

In the Middle-Ages, French Rabbi Salomon Tzarfati "Rashi" from Troyes, a most famous Biblical commentator, was already including French words into his Hebrew sentences, when there was no adequate translation:

> Great biblical scholars like Rashi were using words from local languages written in Hebrew letters to fill in the gaps when the Hebrew language lacked a suitable term or when the reader might not be familiar with the Hebrew term. For example, in his commentary on Gen. 19:28, when Rashi comes across the Hebrew word "*qiytor*" (a word that is not used anywhere else in the Bible), he explains the word by writing, in Hebrew letters, "torche b'la-az" (that is, "*torche* in French").[50]

The meaning of Hebrew "qiytor" is "fumée épaisse, vapeur"[51] in French, "a fume, i.e. cloud:--smoke, vapour", in English.[52]

Mixing languages has been a cultural characteristic, but more than anything else, a life necessity for the Jewish people as they met with new linguistic environments.

---

50   www.Jewfaq.org/yiddish.htm
51   http://www.strong.kabbale.be/strong_hebreu/strong-hebreu-7008.html
      Lexique de l'ancien testament hébreu (et araméen).
52   James Strong. *Hebrew Dictionary. A Concise Dictionary of the Words in the Hebrew Bible, with their Renderings in the Authorized English Version.* 1890. Madison, NJ.
http://www.heraldmag.org/olb/Contents/dictionaries/SHebrew.pdf

Given this plasticity of mind procured to the Jewish people by centuries of hardly voluntary wandering through cultures and their different languages, it seems only natural that, when they immigrated and adopted American English they wished to bring it a touch of Yiddish. As the Yiddish journalist Charles Rappaport once said: "I speak ten languages- all of them in Yiddish"[53]!

It is this "Yiddish touch" that we are now going to analyze in American English documents.

---

[53]   Cited by Léo Rosten in *The joys of Yiddish* (New York: Pocket Book Edition): XVI

Part Two :
Jewish Immigration in America, Yiddish and American English : History of a Meeting

I. Jewish Immigration in America, a Brief Historical Outline

The first Jews to come to America were Spanish fugitives, fleeing from the Inquisition, but how many of them settled is not exactly known. The first indication about a number of Jews in the North America is about 2 500 by 1775.[54]

In 1850 this number had increased to 50 000[55], and in 1870 they were already 250 000[56]. The migrations in the 1840's were essentially caused by the massive pogroms in Ukraine, Russia and Eastern Europe. But the full weight of Jewish immigration to America is yet to come:

> It is conservatively estimated that during the period 1881-1914 almost two million Jewish immigrants had found a haven in the United States. During the later Russian pogrom years of 1903-1906 the annual influx greatly exceeded that of previous years: in 1903: 77 544; 1904: 92388; 1905: 125 234; 1907: 114 932 [...][57]

A witness of the time gives, in 1913, the following description of the Lower East Side:

---

54   http://www.historycentral.com/Revolt/Americans/religion.html

55   Raphael Patai, *Tents of Jacob: the Diaspora – Yesterday and Today* (New Jersey: Prentice-Hall 1971): 334, 361

56   Abram L. Sachar, *A History of the Jews* (New York: Alfred A. Knopf, 1953): 302

57   Nathan Ausubel, *Pictorial History of the Jewish People* (New York : Crown Publishers Inc., 1953, 11th edition 1963): 283

The migration *en masse* of the Jews of Eastern Europe to these highly developed English-speaking countries means something more than a mere change of locality. Though the full significance has hardly yet been appreciated, there is no doubt that this migration is of the very greatest importance for the future of Judaism [...] It is true that the Jewish quarter of New York is little else than a Russian or Galician Ghetto on American soil, and its inmates toil under the sweating system as tailors, cobblers or carpenters for their daily bread; but how long will this be so?"[...]

In New York the great majority of immigrants are concentrated in the East End. This concentration may be put down partly to religions motives (proximity to synagogues and Kosher butchers), though the real reason is undoubtedly that the immigrant Jew - ignorant of the English language and of American life - instinctively seeks intercourse among his own people [...] But in proportion as he learns English and begins to get familiar with American life, he finds the East End with its sweated workroom too narrow for him, and seeks employment outside. The East End serves as a sort of distiller [...][58]

And indeed, the Jew's wish to become part of the mainstream at their arrival in America can easily be deducted from their eagerness to learn English and technical professions, despite

---

[58]   Arthur Ruppin, *The Jews of To-Day* (London: G. Bell and Sons, 1913): 93

difficult conditions, even after an exhausting day's work in the sweatshops. Night classes were held at "the Educational Alliance", the famous settlement house on East Broadway which, for decades, played an important role in the Americanization of East Side immigrants. Thousands of adults "greenhorns" [59] (newcomers in the country) attended night school on the East Side to learn English grammar and pronunciation"[60]. As for the children, they were attending the Educational Alliance (EA) early in the morning, before going to public school.

The more "native" American Jews, who had already been there for decades or centuries, had the desire to foster their coreligionists' integration into the American society out of concern that the presence of a backward and poor looking population would result in a rise of anti-Semitism from the part of the American society. To this end the EA was entirely funded by Jewish philanthropist New Yorkers who sought to accelerate the Jews' integration into American society out of mixed feelings they held towards this very population:

> Comprenons bien le déshonneur ressenti par ces grandes familles juives allemandes, qui voyaient leur respectabilité entachée aux yeux des non-juifs par la présence de ces hordes de miséreux pratiquant un judaïsme médiéval [...] la solution à ce problème était

---

[59]   Nathan Ausubel, *Pictorial History of the Jewish People* (New York: Crown Publishers Inc., 1953, 11th edition 1963): 284
[60]   Corinne Lévitt, *Les Juifs de New York à l'aube du XXIème siècle : communauté juive ou identités juives?* (Paris: Connaissances et Savoirs, 2006): 89-90

une américanisation rapide qui pouvait sauver les uns de la honte, et les autres de la pauvreté.[61]

Despite these mixed feelings described by Corinne Levitt, the Educational Alliance's determining role and benefits for tens of thousands of immigrants cannot be underestimated.

We also find a clear indication of their eagerness to help the Jewish immigrants to quickly assimilate into the American society and language, in the fact that the American Jews, through the Joint Distribution Committee[62], provided the arriving Jewish immigrants with a Yiddish-American-Hebrew dictionary[63]. See the document on next page [64].

---

[61]   Corinne Lévitt, 91

[62]   The American Jewish Joint Distribution Committee is an American association, founded in 1914 and whose primary goal was to help Jews at risk or in need, as were most Jewish European immigrants: http://www.jdc.org/jdc-history/years/1914.aspx

[63]   Alexander Harkavy, *Yiddish- English- Hebrew Dictionary* (New York: Hebrew Publishing Company, 1928).

[64]   Courtesy Shayeh Duvid Klapholz

יידיש - ענגליש - העברעאישער

ווערטערבוך

פון

אלכסנדר הארקאווי.

צווייטע. פארבעסערטע און פארגרעסערטע אויפלאגע.

היברו פאבלישינג קאמפאני,
632-634 בראדווי, ניו יארק.
תרפ״ח.

YIDDISH-ENGLISH-HEBREW

DICTIONARY

BY

ALEXANDER HARKAVY.

SECOND EDITION, IMPROVED AND ENLARGED.

Hebrew Publishing Company,
632-34 Broadway, New York.
1928.

Image 2: a Yiddish-English-Hebrew Dictionary, presented as "A Gift from American Jews through the Joint Distribution Committee".
Translated from Yiddish (in Hebrew characters): "A matoune fun amerikaner yidn dorf dem djoïnt distribushn komitet"

II. Yiddish and American English: History of a Meeting.

As we have seen, the 1880s witness a large wave of Jewish emigration from Eastern Europe. In 1885 the *Yidishes Tageblat*, the first daily Yiddish newspaper in the United States, was created. At the time Englicisms in periodicals correspond to a desire of assimilation.

From the late 19th century to the early 20th century, the Jewish Enlightenment movement spread from Germany to all Europe. Its philosophy was pressing for a wider engagement in the secular world and struggling for emancipation and assimilation into the European society. It is well known that this movement looked upon Yiddish as a low-class language.[65] Still, in 1904, Yiddish was selected as the Jewish national language by a conference of Yiddish writers held in New York City.[66] And in 1908, it was proclaimed as a national language at the Czernowitz Yiddish Language Conference.[67]

By 1917, as a result of the immigration of 2.5 million of Jews in 40 years[68], most of them Yiddish speaking, the Yiddish

---

[65]   Leo Rosten, *The Joys of Yiddish* (Pocket Book, 1970): VIII
[66]   Sol Steinmetz, *Yiddish and English, The story of Yiddish in America* (Tuscaloosa and London: The University of Alabama Press, second edition 2001): 17
[67]   Sol Steinmetz, *Yiddish and English, The story of Yiddish in America* (Tuscaloosa and London: The University of Alabama Press, second edition 2001): 18
[68]   Sol Steinmetz, *Yiddish and English, The story of Yiddish in America* (Tuscaloosa and London: The University of Alabama Press, second edition 2001): 16

language became more and more important in the United States. That is why

In 1919 in New York City, the high density of eastern Jews in the population had made almost every New Yorker familiar with a long list of Yiddish words, e.g. *kosher, shadchan, matzoth, mazuma, yom kippur, meshuggah, gefilte-fisch,* and many non-Jewish New Yorkers have added others that are not generally familiar, e.g. *schul, bar-mitzva, blintzes, kaddish, treyfa, dayyan, goy, dokus, shochet, schmus, shicker, schiksa, mohel, get, hesped, kishkes, kittl, meshummad, and pesach.* The Yiddish exclamation of *oi-yoi* is common New Yorkese, and Yiddish greetings, *mazzal tov* and *scholom aleichim,* are pretty well known and understood.[69]

However, it is only the beginning: by 1920's, one can note "real influx and dissemination of Yiddishisms" when the Yiddish speakers switched to English to blend and "frequently injected into their speech many Yiddish words and expressions, along with Yiddish-influenced intonations, pronunciations, and grammatical constructions". It became common enough in the « mainstream of American English » for scholars to notice it as being culturally significant.[70]

---

[69]   H. L. Mencken, *The American Language* (New York : Alfred A. Knopf, 4th ed., 1936): 216-17. Similar descriptions appear in the earlier editions, the first of which was published in 1919.
[70]   Leo Rosten, *The Joys of Yiddish* (New York: Pocket Book, 1970) V

Indeed from the late 1880's to the late 1920's, Yiddish was "the principal language of American Jews at home and in the streets".[71] By the 1930's, though, "English had become [the] primary language, but Yiddish remained a handy and folksy second language".[72]

This is why, in 1941, the first issue of *Yidishe shprakh*, a New Yorkese Yiddish scholarly journal, deals with the disagreement between the 'purists' (who refuse American English influence on Yiddish) and the 'permissivists' (who welcome American English borrowings).

During World War II, the assimilated American Jews made a first step in the regain of interest about their Jewish roots, and as a result courses in Yiddish <u>were</u> given in universities.[73] And after the war, there was a new mass immigration of Yiddish speakers to the United States.

Around the same time, in 1948, the renascence of Israel created a new interest in the Jewish identity.[74]

Soon after, in 1949, Weinreich's textbook *College Yiddish* was published, and in 1953 Yinglish was already noticed and officially defined as a "Yiddish-English mixture"[75]. Again in 1956, historical events caused the arrival of new Yiddish speakers after the Hungarian revolution. The late 1960's saw

---

[71] Sol Steinmetz, *Yiddish and English, The story of Yiddish in America* (Tuscaloosa and London: The University of Alabama Press, second edition 2001): 17
[72] Sol Steinmetz, *Yiddish and English, The story of Yiddish in America* (Tuscaloosa and London: The University of Alabama Press, second edition 2001): 22
[73] Leo Rosten, *The Joys of Yiddish* (New York: Pocket Book, 1970) V
[74] Sol Steinmetz, *Yiddish and English, The story of Yiddish in America* (Tuscaloosa and London: The University of Alabama Press, second edition 2001): 24
[75] H.J. Gans, "*The 'Yinglish' music of Mickey Katz*", American Quarterly 21 (1953): 442-50, 555-63

another peak of interest for Yiddish. In 1968 Leo Rosten published *The Joys of Yiddish*. Lillian Mermin Feinsilver published *The Taste of Yiddish* in 1970, and Maurice Samuel published in 1971 *In Praise of Yiddish*.

At the same time, according to Stuart Berg Flexner, in 1967, "in the past six years, Yiddish borrowings (*chuzpa, klutz, megillah, shtick*, etc.) have entered in growing numbers".[76]

In 1970, Yinglish was defined as "Yiddish words that are used in colloquial English in both the United States and the United Kingdom".[77]

In 1973, Clarence L. Barnhart noted that "many of these [Yiddish] terms function both as nouns and verbs (*to kvetch, to nosh*), and have also spawned derivatives, such as *klutzy* and *schlocky*."[78] The same year, *The First Jewish Catalog* had six pages about Yiddish.

Three years later, in 1976, *The Second Jewish Catalog* had eight pages about Yiddish.

In 1978, Samuel Rosenbaum's *A Yiddish Word Book For English-Speaking People* contained 2 000 Yiddish words in romanization system.[79]

Soon after, in 1980, *The Third Jewish Catalogue* had twenty five pages about Yiddish.[80]

---

[76] Stuart Berg Flexner, *Preface to the supplement, Dictionary of American Slang*, (New York: Thomas Y. Crowell, 1960, supplemented ed., 1967): 670
[77] Leo Rosten, *The Joys of Yiddish* (Pocket Book, 1970): IX
[78] Clarence L. Barnhart, « On Matters Lexicographical », *American Speach* 45 (1973): 106-7
[79] Leo Rosten, *The Joys of Yiddish* (Pocket Book, 1970): VI
[80] Leo Rosten, *The Joys of Yiddish* (Pocket Book, 1970): VI

In 1982, Leo Rosten's famous *Hooray for Yiddish!* was published along with many imitations.

The end of the Cold War saw another mass emigration of Yiddish speakers to the US.[81]

With the age of the internet, at the end of the 1990s, begin communications among Yiddish speakers and scholars from all around the world, and today

> along with other ethnic groups, the American Jewish community has seen a remarkable renewal of interest in its roots among the Jews who constitute the third-generation descendants of the original immigrants[82].

Contrary to the second generation, they do not believe in the need for the « melting pot ».[83]

Situating our Research in Time

In this research we will concentrate on a time span of sixty years pertaining to the end of the timeline briefly outlined above; we will focus on the second part of the twentieth up to 2009, that is to say from the fifties to today.

To this end we will focus on four periods for which we have collected written sources presenting traces of Yiddish in the American English, and we will analyze a number of primary sources:

---

[81]   Leo Rosten, *The Joys of Yiddish* (Pocket Book, 1970): IX
[82]   Leo Rosten, *The Joys of Yiddish* (Pocket Book, 1970): IX
[83]   Sol Steinmetz, *Yiddish and English, The story of Yiddish in America* (Tuscaloosa and London: The University of Alabama Press, second edition 2001): 24

First period: the years 1950-1960, in New York City, more precisely in the Lower East Side. The sources will be signs and fronts of Jewish shops.

Second period: the years 1970. The source will be a book edited in 1971: *"A Bintel Brief". Sixty Years of Letters from the Lower East Side to the Jewish Daily Forward.* The introduction and foreword to the book, dated 1971, provide us with a direct insight into an English corpus dated of the 1970's, mixed with quite a lot of Yiddish words and phrases. As for the letters' translation, it will inform us about which Yiddish terms remained untranslated, thus signaling an assumed understandability from the part of a reader of such a book in the years 1970.

Third period: the years 2003-2009. The source for this period will consist of extracts of *The Forward* in English version.

Fourth period: today. The years 2008-2009. The source for this period will consist in extracts from Jewish websites, forums and chats on the internet.

Part Three:
Yiddish and
Contemporary English

I. First Period: the Years 1950-1960. Jewish Shops in the Lower East Side.

1. Description of the source and its historical context

The signs and shop windows of the Jewish shops in the Lower East Side, where the Jewish immigrants lived *en masse* a century ago, provide us with such traces. The importance of Yiddish as the Jewish immigrants' main language cannot be overrated in the first decades of the 20th century: *"En 1930 [...] 1 750 000 juifs américains déclarent le yiddish comme leur langue maternelle et usuelle »*[84]. Knowing that "three quarters of all East European Jews who arrived during the flood-tide of Jewish immigration lived for a while on the Lower East Side in New York"[85], we can today only imagine the historic pregnancy of Yiddish in the immigrants' new life on the Lower East Side.

A reminder of the uniqueness of this place to Jewish immigration, the following shop signs are but a remnant of what has been the centre of Jewish daily life in New York at the beginning and in the middle of the 20th century.

As we will now see, these old signs already illustrate a degree of melting.

---

[84]   Jean Baumgarten, Rachel Ertel, et al., *Les pôles de la vie ashkénaze après 1945*, in *Mille ans de cultures ashkénazes*. (Paris : Liana Lévi, 1994): 584
[85]   Arthur Ruppin. *The Jews of To-Day*. (London: G. Bell and Sons, 1913): 283

The first picture shows the sign of the shop of "Zelig Blumenthal". As the following extracts inform us:

Zelig Blumenthal is one of the few remaining Judaica shops on Essex Street, between Grand and East Broadway, which used to be dominated by small stores that catered to the needs of the Lower East Side's Jewish community.[86]

In 1950, Rabbi Zelig Blumenthal, a seventh generation Yerushalmi, came to New York City from Jerusalem, Israel. In New York, he saw that there was a growing demand to supply synagogues with beautiful Torah scrolls. Remembering the workmanship from the old generations, he decided to supply the traditional quality from the old city. Rabbi Blumenthal's reputation, as a soifer (scribe) of the highest quality, spread rapidly. In a neighborhood of scribes, located in the Lower East Side of New York, he became known as a "scribe's scribe", one who followed the laws and customs of one's heritage[87].

[86]   http://www.immigrantheritagetrail.org/?q=node/401
[87]   http://www.torahsplus.com/about.asp

Picture 1: the shop of Zelig Blumenthal on Essex Street

The second, third, fourth and fifth pictures show shop signs which are also situated in the Lower East Side on Essex Street.

Picture 2: shop sign situated on Essex Street

Picture 3: shop sign situated on Essex Street

Picture 4: shop sign situated on Essex Street

Picture 5: sign of Weinfeld's shop on Essex Street

The sixth and seventh pictures show the storefront of a shop situated on East Houston Street, the Yonah Schimmel's Knish Bakery:

> About 1890 Yonah Schimmel, a Jewish immigrant and part-time Hebrew teacher, used a pushcart to start his knish bakery on the Lower East Side, New York's traditional home to new immigrants. When business expanded, Yonah and his cousin, Joseph Berger, rented

a small store on Houston Street. Two years later Yonah returned to teaching Hebrew, while Joseph and his wife (Yonah's daughter, Rose) took over the business, retaining the original name. In 1910 the Bergers moved the business to the opposite side of Houston Street, where it remains to this day, still under the family's management[88]

We have two pictures of this shop, one from the fifties as it is taken from a book published in 1953:

Picture 6: "A recent photograph of Yonah Shimmel's Knishery"

[88]   The New York City Museum, http://www.mcny.org/museum-collections/painting-new-york/pttcat109.htm

and the other dating from the years 2000:

Picture 7: Yonah Shimmel's Knishery nowadays (years 2000)

For these shop signs, we will thus be able to analyze the evolution between the two states of language displayed by these two pictures distant from some 50 years.

2. Linguistic Analysis

a. The Vocabulary

We can see on the first three pictures the phrase "Bar Mitzvah Sets". People used to go to someone who wove and sold tallisim for the tallis (prayer shawl), to a sofer (scribe) for the tefillin (phylacteries)... There were no general stores, but many craftsmen selling their own products.

The "bar mitzvah set" may have been a new concept, which started being a common in America. This would explain the juxtaposition of "bar mitzvah" and "set", Yiddish and English.

On the second picture, we see that "Tallis" has been replaced by its translation: "Prayer Shawl". It could be because the owner couldn't decide on the spelling, as we notice on the other pictures that this word seems to be spelled in many different ways ("taliesim", "taleisim", "talaisem" ...). Unless the owner felt that most of the customers weren't so fluent in Yiddish as all plurals but one are English, and the rather well-known word "Sofer" is translated ("scribe").

On the third picture, we notice that the last line is made of a Yiddish word, "kipas", between parentheses, and its translation "skull caps" on the left. As most Yiddish words on this sign take an English plural, we can suppose that the people shopping there were better acquainted with English than with Yiddish, or that the shopkeepers wanted to appear more American.

On the fourth picture, the sign advertises for "Porochasen Torah mantles", and "Talaisem [made of] silk & wool". Since all the plurals are Yiddish, it is interesting that they choose to translate "porochasn" as "Torah mantle", but without substituting it to its translation. It could be because the word "poroches" (plural "porochasn") was unknown to people not heavily involved in the Jewish cult, yet some people may not be able to understand the translation as they were not fluent enough in English, and needed the Yiddish version to understand.

As for Picture Five, we find a balance between Yiddish and American terms as far as one item is concerned: "skull caps" / "yarmulkas". One can note that it is the English term which is more emphasized (in terms of the letters' size).

b. Morphological Features

Plural Marks

On the pictures, we can notice that some of the words that have become the most common in English (compared to the other words) have often been "anglicized" to the point of taking the English plural marks instead of the original Yiddish one.

Indeed, on the first picture, we see "Torah*s*" instead of "Tor*os*" and "Mezuzah*s*" instead of "Mezuz*os*". The relatively well-known words "Torah" and "mezuzah" take an English plural. But less common words like "tefillin" and "taleisim" don't; instead they retain their original Aramaic "-in" (feminine plural) and Hebrew "-im" (masculine plural) endings.

On the second picture, we notice "Sefer *Torahs*" instead of "Sifrei (for "sefarim") Torah" (in Yiddish, when there is a compound word, the one bearing the plural mark is the one whose number is modified – here the word "sefer", meaning "scroll", not the one describing what kind of scroll it is). It can probably be explained because the well-known word is "sefer Torah", the singular, and the plural "sifrei", being irregular, would confuse many people.

The more common words "Menorah*s*" (instead of "Menor*os*") and "Mezuza*s*" (instead of "Mezuz*os*") take an English plural, as we saw in the first part.

On the third picture, we can see that "Taliesim" is a Yiddish plural, but again we see "Sefer Torah*s*" instead of "Sifrei Torah" (see second picture), and "Kipa*s*" instead of "Kip*os*".

On the fourth picture, we don't notice one single English plural on a borrowed word: "Tfilin" (phylactery worn by men during the morning prayer, from Hebrew "tefila"; the plural is in fact the Aramaic fem. plural mark: –"in"), "Mzuzaus" (from "mezuzah", "door lintel", word used to designate the scroll fixed to the lintel at the doors of the Jewish homes), "Yarmilkes" (from "yarmulke", the traditional cap), "Talaisem", Taleisim" (both from "talis", "cape", the prayer shawl). It could be totally arbitrary, but the general appearance of the shop tells us that it is probably older than the other shops, and it is quite possible that at that time the signs were made in Hebrew. Yiddish words were really less integrated and well-known than today. It is interesting to note that these forms are rather "exotic" (even for the considered corpus) - for example, "mzuzaus" has not been found elsewhere, it is a onetime occurrence. We believe that with this quite original plural mark, the author tried to convey the diphthongization (the fact of turning a single-articulation vowel in a double-articulation one) of the Yiddish pronunciation. The Hebrew phoneme /o/ is diphthongized in Yiddish as /oi/ when followed by a consonant. As the phoneme /oi/ can be transliterated by "au" in German, the author, who has probably learned the Latin alphabet through German, found natural to write /mzuzois/ that way. Since these features have been maintained for numerous decades now, maybe the owner did not feel the necessity to update his window; this is to say that the shop probably does cater to this day to old, religious, Yiddish-speaking people.

On the fifth picture, and in sharp contrast with the preceding one, all the plural marks are English plurals with "s", whether the word be English or Yiddish: "skull caps" / "yarmulkas; this tends to show a trend towards Americanization.

Concerning the last two pictures of Yonah Shimmel's shop, and the evolution having occurred in the time span of some 50 years, the following remarks can be made:

The first picture, from the fifties, conveys an impression of unfamiliarity with the typical American sign shop as it states: "Here is the original…"; it is not the case anymore on the second picture.

On the old picture, both English and Yiddish are featured (equally sized) on the shop's window. And so the Hebrew characters of Yiddish retain an important place, which is no more the case in the second picture where it has disappeared altogether.

The concerned item ("knish") remains untranslated on the two shop signs, as it represents a very specific kind of food: as explained on the website of New York City's Museum, "the knish, a specialty of Eastern European Jews, has, like other ethnic foods, permeated the diets of many immigrant groups" [...] traditional knishes consist of boiled buckwheat groats or mashed potatoes wrapped with dough, then baked and served hot"[89].

In the first picture, "knishe" takes an "-e" as it qualifies the noun "bakery"- thus with a Yiddish adjective ending[90]; on the contrary, the more recent sign shop just uses "knish", following English grammar rules, without the –e agreement ending. As a last remark the more recent picture features the word "knishes", thus with an English plural, which was not the case on the former one. On the whole, the evolution of Yonah Shimmel's shop signs shows a strong Americanization by using less Yiddish and more English than the others.

We can draw a number of conclusions from this first analysis:
- From start, Yiddish words found their way into American English;
- Yiddish words often became Americanized, just like those who chose to spell them with English features;
- There is some doubt about the English written form to assign to some religious items (for example "taliesim", "taleisim", "talaisem"; but also "mezuzahs", "mezuzas", "mzuzaus";

---

[89]   http://www.mcny.org/museum-collections/painting-new-york/pttcat109.htm

[90]   in Yiddish, as in German, the adjective agrees in gender and number with the affected noun

"yarmulkas", "yarmilkes", …); at the same time, we note a sometimes inaccurate spelling of English words (like "Specialty", on picture 3); these clues attest of a degree of "linguistic disorientation" from the part of the shop owners. Although most of the shop owners are themselves immigrants, we can't neither interpret these ways of writing just as being signs of a difficulty to adopt the new language, nor just as a hesitation regarding the linguistic competences of the public catering to their shop. A mix of both reasons is probably the best explanation;

- Nevertheless and from start, different positions (whether conscious or not) are being taken by the authors: to insert a Yiddish touch into English, to assimilate, to "Americanize" the Yiddish words (by way of translation, of adding English plurals to the Yiddish words, etc.); or, on the contrary, to "keep" one's culture and language, to maintain the Yiddish words, or endings, even to "radicalize" the "exotic", "non-American", original pronunciation. The choices opened to the immigrant when he came to America, are to this day reflected on these shop signs.

II Second Period; the 1970s: *A Bintel Brief*, Foreword, Introduction and English Translation.

1. Description of the Source and Historical Context

These letters, written from 1906 to 1967 in Yiddish, were translated and published by Isaac Metzker under the title *A Bintel Brief* which means "a bundle of letters" in Yiddish. Born in 1900 in Galicia, Poland, Isaac Metzker arrived in the United States of America in 1924. The foreword is by Harry Golden, born in Galicia, Poland in 1902, who arrived in New York City in 1905. At the end of the book we find a glossary, and foreign words are in italics. The introduction and foreword to the book provide us with a direct insight into English texts of the 1970's, mixed with quite a lot of Yiddish words and locutions. They are themselves sources for investigating on the use of Yiddish in American English.

As for the letters translation, we believe that we can make use of this corpus by analyzing which Yiddish terms were translated into English by Isaac Metzker, and which ones remained in Yiddish. We presume this will allow us to see which Yiddish words were assumed to be understood by the reader of such a book in the 1970s.

2. Linguistic Analysis of the Introduction and Foreword

a. The Vocabulary

In the **introduction** by Isaac Metzker, one already finds several Yiddish words.

(page 8) "There, crowded together, they stayed near *landsleit* who had migrated before them."

"Landsleit" designates a fellow from the same town or village in Yiddish. This word is not so commonly heard today, but as it is not translated it was probably easily understandable in the 1970s. It is interesting to note that the word becomes rarer and rarer in the letters as time passes. The association of this word with the memories of the hardships in the old country probably accelerated its disappearance.

(page 8) "The transition from the old way of life in the *shtetel* to a new life in the seething, vast city of New York was not an easy one to make."

The "shtetel", a small town with a heavily Jewish population, is a Yiddish concept and as such is rarely translated. It may also be that first generation immigrants did not translate it for similar reasons as the aforementioned word "Landsleit". The direct translation of "shtetel" would be "small town", but it would lack the "old country" and "Jewish" connotations.

(page 10) "It was as if their *Alef-Beis* from home and *kheyder* had followed them to America".

"Alef-Beis", the Yiddish word for "alphabet", and "kheyder", the Yiddish word for "religious primary school", could have been translated, but both have a strong connotation attached to them, especially for first generation Jewish immigrants, and these "childhood and way of life in the old country nostalgia" connotations would just not be properly rendered by the American English translations.

(page 16) "One reader writes that his asking for an opinion and counsel from the editor reminds him of the way people went to the *rebbe* in the old country".

A "rebbe", could be translated as "Chassidic community leader". It also has its own connotation for Chassidic Jews. A "rebbe" is not only the religious leader, but the advisor, the third-party in case of a quarrel, and in some communities he was even considered as a potential Messiah.

In Harry Golden's **foreword**, one can read:

(page 20) "The mother made the new husband learn Hebrew and he had to pray every morning wearing his *yarmulka*". A "yarmulka" is a skull cap worn by observant Jewish men, at least during prayer time. The word is kept as it is, probably, because it is very common for the (Jewish) reader of the time.

(page 21) "The Jewish fathers and brothers came to America first and worked to earn enough for a *shiff's carte* (steamship passage)." Nowadays, the word "steamship passage" is almost never found in Yiddish as it is an outdated concept, except when referring to first generation immigrants.

Indeed, in Eastern Europe, the "shiff's carte" was a concept of its own, a ticket for the land of freedom and security[91] (quite like today's green card), and not just a mere "steamship passage". Using the American English term would not convey this connotation of a foreigner's point of view.

(page 23) "Ghetto humour was usually in the form of the *vitz*, a philosophical witticism, or a *vitzl*, its diminutive, which was a little joke or pun". Here, the writer found it necessary to include a reformulation in order to explain the Yiddish term because it is not a very common word.

b. Morphological Features

Yiddish Patterns, Bound Morphology and Bi-lingual Words

(page 9) "They went to work on the Sabbath, they shaved their beards, and many of them began to eat non-*kosher* foods." While "shabbes", the Jewish day of rest, has a well-known English translation, "Sabbath", "kosher" (fit for consumption according to Jewish law) does not have one, and thus cannot be translated even if the author is totally Americanized. The

---

[91]   In a review for the 1939 Yiddish movie "A Brivele der Mamen" ("A small letter to Mama"), we can find the phrase: "When Dovid, a pitiful figure, finally goes off to America to escape the humiliation of being seen as such a loser by everybody except Dobrish in the little home town, it is Max, who empties out the family savings from a jar in the kitchen <u>to pay for his "shiff-karte" -- Passage to the Promised Land</u> of Amerika."
http://www.fest21.com/blog/alexdeleon/a_brivele_der_mamen_a_little_letter_to_mama

word "non-kosher" has been formed on the English model "non + hyphen + something", meaning according to the Merriam-Webster dictionary "lacking the usual especially positive characteristics of the thing specified", which is why only the Yiddish component is in italics. In Yiddish, the negation is rarely used. When possible, a new word is found, even if it is not the *exact* opposite. Something that is not kosher is called "treif". This word coming from Hebrew word "taref" (meaning "torn") is used in the Bible to designate a decaying carcass, which cannot be eaten according to Jewish dietary laws. Since then, it has taken the extended sense of "not kosher". In the example above, it is interesting to note that the author did not use the Yiddish word "treif" (which is quite technical) and replaced it with a new word, "non-kosher" which is also based on Yiddish but is easier to understand.

(page 25) "If a newcomer was a *singleman* (unmarried), he was often introduced speedily to the *shadkhan* (marriage broker)." Here we find another mixed word, built on a Yiddish pattern: a "yingerman" is a "man" who is "ying" ("young"), so a "singleman" is a man who is single. Indeed, this word is in italics, as if it was foreign, because in a way it is. It works even better since the word "man" has the same meaning in American English and in Yiddish. Indeed, since English and Yiddish are both Germanic languages, they have common points that make mixings much easier. Both "foreign" words are treated the same way: they are in italics, and followed by a definition between parentheses. But interestingly, since "singleman" is built with English components (although on a

Yiddish pattern), the author did not feel the need to include it in the glossary.

Plural Marks and Suffixes

(page 24) "How would you accumulate the necessary quota of *mitsves,* good deeds to be added upon the day of reckoning?". "Mitsves", the plural of "mitsva", "good deed", was also probably no longer familiar enough, especially under its plural form, to be left without an explanation in 1971.

(page 24) "And the *schnorrers,* the professional beggars of the ghetto, how they elevated their "work" to a fine art! [...] The greatest case of a true *schnorrer,* the essence of *schnorrer*dom, involved me personally not many years ago". It seems that in 1971 the word "schnorrer" was no longer familiar enough to not include an explanation about it. It must be noted that the plural form, here, is an English one, and not a Yiddish one. This type of endings must have been already rather common, as the whole word is in italics, while another, less common, suffix, would have been seen as "not Yiddish" and left in plain text. As for the English suffix –dom, it is not common enough on a Yiddish word to be written in italics. The word "*schnorrer*dom" (note the difference between the italics and the plain text) shows a possibility of construction of mixed words: any word in a given language seems to be able to receive any suffix from another language, as long as it makes sense. It is even possible that the writer made up the word.

Indeed, after research, only one other occurrence of the word was found[92].

On the whole, one must note that the persistence of Yiddish features (terms, morphological marks) in the 1971 book's introduction and foreword is relatively scarce. Although the introduction and the foreword were written by two different authors, the way these sentences, phrases and words are used are not different: while often the non-translated words are very well-known, like "kosher", sometimes they are simply words that the writer found no real equivalent for.

Also a touch of nostalgia pervades the choice of the retained Yiddish words, often relating to the "old world": the "shtetel" with the "landsleit", the "rebbe" which used to teach the children in the "kheyder"...

Many of the integrated sentences also retain these "untranslatable" words, but sometimes, whether the goal is to teach the reader the concerned word, or whether the writer has assumed it will no more be recognized by the reader, the Yiddish word will is found together with an explanation. From these examples, we can also see how new, bi-lingual words were created and this is possible to such an extended point thank the similarity of Yiddish and English. New terms which

---

[92]   The occurrence was found in a blog entry entitled "The Scottish Schnorrocracy: Christie Davies visits Scotland - and discovers a country ruled by schnorrers": "We can see in this incident both the height to which the gallant Scots can rise and the cause of their almighty fall to schnorrerdom." Interestingly, the blog entry contains many other "schnorrer based" words, like "schnorrocracy", the rule of the schnorrer, and "Euroschnorrers", European schnorrers.

    http://www.socialaffairsunit.org.uk/blog/archives/001566.php

will be understood by analogy, like in the case of "yingerman" / "singleman" as described above, can be easily created.

3. The Immigrants' letters, Translation's Analysis

a. The Vocabulary

(page 41) "Meanwhile, I had a baby and had to make the *bris* alone" (letter dated 1906). "bris" is Yiddish for the Jewish ceremony of circumcision. It was either left untranslated because the word was well-known, or because the English translation "circumcision" does not totally convey the idea of the whole ceremony as one of extreme religious significance, but of a medical act routinely done in the United States of America.

(page 74) "He pays a pious man to say *kaddish* prayer for the dead, and he burns a *yohrzeit* candle in his home" " (letter dated 1908). The "kaddish" is the Jewish prayer for the dead, and the "yohrzeit" is the anniversary of the death. These words imply religious ceremonies that the American English words wouldn't convey well without a periphrasis or in-depth explanation, hence the non-translation.

(page 75) "Dudja Silverberg [a very pious Jew] goes to *shul* to speak with God, I go to *shul* to speak with Dudja" (letter dated 1908)

The word "shul" means "synagogue". It was probably not translated as it was still well-known[93].

b. Morphological Features

The phenomena most frequently retrieved concern plural marks, suffixes, Yiddish patterns and bi-lingual words.

The earliest trace of mixing, in this book, would be the word "alrightniks", found on page 140 in a letter dating back to 1920. An "alrightnik" is a person whose life is "all right", someone who succeeded. The word is composed of the American English phrase "all right", and the Yiddish / Slavic origin[94] agentive suffix "-nik". This word, based on an American English word, is not found in the glossary, and is not in italics: it does not seem to be considered foreign. But like all the previous examples, it is not translated and was already found in the original, Yiddish version, hence the quotation marks. It shows that, in 1920, there were already mixings, and they happened often enough to find them in a letter to a serious, well-known paper.

(page 88) "A *Verein* doctor would call on the sick man and look around his house of three children and his pregnant wife and what could he tell him?" Here, the phrase "Verein doctor", composed of a Yiddish and an American English word, is even more natural to use since the Yiddish word for "doctor", "Doktor", is extremely close to the American English one.

---

[93] We will see that this is no longer the case in the more recent corpus (the *Forward*'s articles from the years 2000

[94] Ellen F. Prince, *Yiddish as a Contact Language*, in « Creolization and Contact », Creole Language Library Volume 23, edited by Norval Smith and Tonjes Veenstra (University of Amsterdam-Free University Berlin, 2001, vi, 323 pp): 265

Indeed, the full Yiddish phrase would have been "Verein Doktor". "Verein" means "[trade] union".

On page 101, we find two Yiddish words taking an English plural: "I was born in a small town in Russia, and until I was sixteen I studied in *Talmud Torahs* and *yeshivas*, but when I came to America I changed quickly". The Yiddish plurals would have been "Talmudei Torah" and "yeshivos", but here the translator probably thought the words would be more easily understood with an English plural, especially since the first word is a compound word and thus takes a plural mark that readers who were not very much acquainted with Yiddish would not understand. Also, the translator described himself as a "freethinker", which means he considers himself to be as much Americanized as possible, hence the American English plurals. When he published this book, he had been living in the United States of America for 47 years!

On page 117: "They did not sit *shive* even though they had lost a child". "Shive", meaning "seven" in Yiddish (from Hebrew "sheva", seven), is the time of heavy mourning in the Jewish tradition. As its name indicates, it lasts seven days. The melted verb "to sit shive" means mourning in the Jewish way. The Yiddish verb, "shive sitzen", translates exactly as "to sit shive". Also, the English equivalent "going into mourning" would not give the idea of the traditional Jewish mourning rituals.

On the whole, the examples of retained Yiddish words and other morphological features in the translation of the letters, prove equally scarce; this witnesses to a state of discourse which will retain the somewhat "untranslatable" Yiddish way of life, customs and experience, but will rather opt for a maximal integration into the English language and way of life.

We are now going to see how this blending has evolved in more recent sources.

III. Third Period: the Years 2003-2009. *The Forward* in English Version.

1. Description of the source and historical context

In 1987, after many deceases among the first-generation immigrants, the number of Yiddish mother tongue readers has decreased, but at the same time, with a perceived need to retain something of the Jewish American culture and heritage which had been there for almost one century, an English version of the Forward came to light: The *Jewish Daily Forward.* It has been there ever since.

In order to search for traces of Yiddish features in the newspaper's articles, we have carried out an extensive investigation into the online Archives of the *Forward* in English, which start in 2003. Out of the 200 consulted articles, only 29 showed any sign of Yiddish presence whatsoever[95]. And even if the newspaper does reflect an amount of Yiddish features, which will be described below, one is stricken by the repetitive aspect of these traces and their relative poverty.

In the analysis below, we will consider the following points:

> •in which type of articles these Yiddish features are present,
>
> •which Yiddish features are present in the articles (words, phrases, morphological features, syntactic ones).

---

[95] The main extracts of the articles are available upon request.

2. Linguistic Analysis

A classification of the articles following their rubric of origin shows that, very logically, the community news and the reader's column, together with the "cultural" articles and "The Schmooze" (itself being a mix of community and cultural news), are the most impacted as they make up for 21 out of the 29 articles with Yiddish features involved.

The most "productive" rubrics and subjects for the triggering of Yiddish features are indeed (going by descendant order):

The "News" (here meaning Jewish community's news), community affairs, with 7 articles:

Orthodox Union Promises New Openness, January 03, 2003, by Alana Newhouse

Scholars Ask, What Would the Rav Do, January 03, 2003, by Alana Newhouse

Lobbyist's New restaurants Put the 'K' in K Street, January 03, 2003, by Ori Nir

Only in America: Building Bridges at a Unique Seder, May 2, 2003, by Andrea Barron

High Cost of Living Leads Orthodox To Look Beyond Borders of New York, March 28, 2008, by Anthony Weiss

Grandparents Circle in on Continuity, September 12, 2008, by Rebecca Spence

On the Jersey Waterfront, Jews Return, But Jewish Community Still Struggles, April 24, 2009, by Anthony Weiss

The Reader's column/ Bintel Brief, with 5 articles:

Letter to the edition: *Who wears the Pants?* January 03, 2003

The Bintel Brief. Dr. Ruth on *Beshert* Troubles, May 21, 2007

The Bintel Brief. *Help! Our 6-Year-Old Son is More Observant Than we Are*, February 9, 2009, by Ayelet Waldman

The Bintel Brief. *How Do I Stop My Dad From Feeding Ham to My Kosher Son?* February 23, 2009, by Ayelet Waldman

The Bintel Brief. *Help! My Adult Daughter's a Schnorrer*, March 15, 2009 by Jeffrey Zaslow

<u>Subjects relating to Arts, music, culture</u>, with 5 articles:

Tango: Not Jewish, But Not 100% Not Jewish, June 10, 2005, by Alexander Gelfand

Remembering How the Yiddish Theater Turned Into Broadway, June 09, 2006, by Alexander Gelfand

The Anti-'Fiddler, October 19, 2007, by Alexander Gelfand

Hasidic Rabbi by Day, Pop Artist by Night, February 22, 2008, by Sara Trappler Spielman

Songs of a Lost Tribe's Longing, September 12, 2008, by Joseph Leichman

The rubric "The Shmooze", with 4 articles:

Workmen's Circle Seder Hits High Note, May 02, 2003, by Masha Leon

Rabbi, Can You Spare a Dime? Coping With Hard Times in a Town That Was Just Getting By, May 30, 2003, by Lisa Keys

2nd Ave Deli Cooks Up Controversy, February 22, 2008, by Gabriel Sanders

Chabon and Waldman: The Couple That Kvells Together, September 12, 2008, By Marissa Brostoff

The rubric "Fast Forward" ("a leading window into the lifestyles of younger Jews"[96]), with 4 articles:
The Stove's On – It Must Be Chicken in the Pot, May 2, 2003
Uneasy Reading: Books About Parenting Fall Flat. The East Village Mamele, September 24, 2004, by Marjorie Ingall
Confirmation: The Life and Times of a Modern Ritual, June 10, 2005, by Jenna Weissman Joselit
A Prison Shul, Lost and Found, April 07, 2009, by Devra Ferst
The Editorial, with 2 articles:
Recipe for Desunion, January 31, 2003
Seder with the Obamas, April 24, 2009
Der Yiddish-Vinkl. A Weekly Briefing on the Mother Tongue, with 2 articles:
May 02, 2003, & May 30, 2003.
The Forward Forum, with one article:
Family Reunion at Home Plate, May 30, 2003, by Leonard Fein

Although three names do feature plain Yiddish: "The Shmooze" (Yiddish "schmusn", from Hebrew "schmu'ot", "rumors"), The East Village *Mamele* (Yiddish for "mommy"), and Der Yiddish-Vinkl ("Corner"), we will see that these rubrics do not present many Yiddish features.

The Vocabulary
What is characteristic of this source is the fact that more often than not, the Yiddish terms will be in italics and will almost

---

systematically be accompanied by their English translation, thus anticipating their non-comprehension by the reader.[97]
From a semantic point of view, the subjects triggering the presence of Yiddish terms are essentially related to:
Affirmation of plain Jewish existence:
Yidishkait ("[...] a little closer to *yidishkayt*") - in italics as the word is not deemed common, and with the following explanation: "[...] they may want to be a little closer to God."
Religious issues:
Issur (in italics, with a translation: "prohibition")
Tchotchkes (in italics, left untranslated)
Shiurs (in italics, with a translation: "[...] *shiurs,* or lessons [...]", and with a -s English plural mark)
Da'as Torah in italics)
Daven, in italics
Halakhic, Halachic
Droshe (in italics as the word is not common)
"*Baruch hashems*" (in italics as the expression is not common; with an English plural mark)
Kapores: in italics, with a definition, and even a reminder of the concerned language: Yiddish (!): "[...] the venerable atonement ritual of *kapparot* (*kapores* in Yiddish)").
"*Khazones*", with translation: "[...] Jewish music both sacred and secular, from klezmer to *khazones* (synagogue chant) [...]"
Frum

---

[97] For the words left untranslated, see the Glossary in the Appendix

"*shul*" (in italics and in proximity context with the Englis
equivalent: "[…] recent efforts to restore the <u>synagogue</u>
which is believed to be the first prison *shul* in the country")
<u>Jewish rites and holidays:</u>
 (related to Passover): "Seder", "Matzo", "Haggada", "Sede
plates", "Passover Seder" (translated as the reader is no
considered as knowing what is a seder), "box of matzo"
"matzo balls"
(related to Hanoucah): "Dreidel", "Hanukkah menorah"
"Hanukkah party", "an annual event called Hanukkah"
Minyan
Yeshiva, "*rosh yeshiva*," with italics and translation: "yeshiv
head"
shabbos
shul
bris (the general and very repetitive context orients the reade
towards the translation: "[…] It was a great privilege to brin
a son to be <u>circumcised</u> into the covenant of Abraham").
Mikvah
bar mitzvah
"*Kiddush*" (italics)
Yarzheit
<u>Religious objects and features:</u>
Yarmulke
Sets of tefillin
Mezuza
Chasidic garb
Tzitzit
<u>Food:</u>

"Kosher"

"Shmaltz" ("The chicken's fat, or *shmaltz*, became the chief frying agent");

"Gribenes" ("[…] the skin was rendered into the delicious cracklings known as gribenes")

"Heldzl" ("[…] the neck, or *heldzl*, served as a casing to be stuffed […]")

Family:

Haimish (left untranslated, but not the analogy of the Yiddish and English root, a clue for understanding as they are placed side by side: "[…] a nice middle-class, haimish home")

"Kosher home"

"Zayde and *bubbe"*, with translation integrated: "[…] Grandma and Grandpa (I'm guessing these folks aren't going by *Zayde* and *Bubbe*) […]"

Cultural, historical terms:

"Shtetl life"

"Badkhn", with reformulation preceding ("[…] a narrator, the *Badkhn* […]"

"Klezmer", "Klezmer *freilach"*

"[…] the Workmen's Circle/Arbeter Ring […]", note the order with translation preceding.

Greetings, other idiomatic expressions:

"Mazel tov" (the italics shows the expression is not judged common)

"Khas v'shalom", *"Chas v'chalila"* (in italics, left untranslated)

"Bubbe stories" (italics as the word "bubbe" –grandmother- is no more considered common)

"Oy" ("Your father and his wife are feeding your Orthodox child ham? Oy […]"

Human types, qualities, feelings:

Rebbe, "rabbi": the author even manages to put in the translation of the word "rebbe": "[…] Lubavitcher rebbe Rabbi Menachem Mendel Schneerson […]"

Havurah (in italics andwith an explanation): "[…] a social experience, a *havurah* experience with other Jewish people not necessarily as part of a religious group."

Schmendrik, shmendrik, with a qualification hinting at the word's signification:

"[…] the neurotic *shmendrik* […]"

"Goyim"

"*Shikkurs*" (in italics as the word is rare, left untranslated; the plural mark is English)

Mamzer (left untranslated)

Schnorrer, with translation added: "*[…]* a real *schnorrer* — cheapskate."

"*Beshert* ", with translation ("[…] the issue of *beshert*, or soul mates […]")

"*Seykhl*" (in italics and with a definition): "[…] the wit and wisdom that distinguishes *seykhl* from ordinary intelligence […]"

Tsores, in italics

Chutzpah

To "kvell" (left untranslated, meaning "to be happy", "to rejoice")

Geshmak, in italics and translated: "delicious"

Body parts:

Tukhes, for "bottom" (left untranslated, unformal)
Pupik ("navel", left untranslated)

On the whole concerning the lexicon, we note that:
- the main bulk of Yiddish words is logically related to religious issues, objects, and feasts;
- we note very few words pertaining to the "old world" (the life in Europe)
- interestingly enough, the lexical fields of human types and qualities are very present;
- some Yiddish words remain untranslated: we think that at least a number of them was not translated for decency reasons (and not particularly religious ones), because they are very informal, sometimes being insults, like "mamzer", (bastard), "shikkur" (drunk); or slang, like "tukhes" (bottom), "pupik" (navel).

Morphological Features
The plural endings are systematically English plural –s endings:

"Talmud Torahs", "mikvehs", "menorahs", "Haggadahs", "Mitzvahs", "Brises", "Dreidels", "Yids" ("Jews"), "Yeshiva *bachers*"; moreover "bachers" is translated ("So many yeshiva *bachers* [boys]…").

The plural marks are indeed simple morphological markers which could have featured a minimal Yiddish presence in the texts. But the whole system of plural marks is English, as the

Yiddish/ Hebrew plural ending would probably make the word too different from the one readers are used to.

Most strikingly, there is not one single morphological reminder of Yiddish in the whole corpus. This comes in sharp difference with the preceding sources (the shop signs and the 1971 book) and will come in even sharper difference in comparison with the internet sources we will see in the following part. This state of discourse points definitely to a "frozen" state of language, which no longer makes it possible to "juggle" with one's linguistic references.

Syntactic features

The poverty of Yiddish-influenced syntactic features in the corpus is a confirmation of the above remark. The sole example of a well-known Yiddish inversion syntactic pattern found in this corpus is the following:

"[…] a spirited discussion about whether a restaurant open on the Sabbath can still be considered kosher. After a correspondent posed the question to Bruni, the food critic wrote a blog post inviting readers to weigh in.

And weigh in they did."

Apart from this example, and for the whole corpus, we were able to note but five creative Yiddish-inspired expressions:

"The hole in the bagel"

to "auction off the matzo" ("Nice to have a president who doesn't auction off the matzo").

"to be kosher" ("I have been kosher about as long as I can remember […]", "My Kosher Son") "a tempest in a *tchainik* (a teapot)"

"a pain in the tush" (familiar, for "bottom").

And for the entire corpus we found no more than a dozen Yiddish-based idiomatic expressions:

He "does his shtick" ("[...] his sons compose and play music, and he does his shtick, complete with song and dance [...]")

"Class and shtick" ("There was class and shtick at the Folksbiene Yiddish Theatre [...]")

"Eat treif"

"Keeping kosher"

"Keep Shabbat"

"Sit shiva".

On the whole for this source, and bearing in mind that we worked on an extensive corpus[98], we can say that these extracts represent therefore the "quintessence" of whatever Yiddish-origin features can be found in the *Forward* for the period 2003-2009. The poverty of this corpus is striking: the retrieved patterns are systematically the same, the found vocabulary is poor; indeed, the Yiddish words and features seem to assume a function of merely reminding the reader of a dim Yiddish "presence" or point of view, more than being part of a living, dynamic process of language. The massive utilization of italics and translations conveys the same impression of a culture striving and going to great pedagogical lengths in order to transmit to its readers at least some remnants of Yiddish language and culture.

---

[98] Some 200 articles were consulted; out of these, 29 articles were selected at first encounter with one Yiddish feature whatsoever, including the features already encountered - that is to say, including redundant vocabulary from the start.

IV. Fourth Period: American Jewish Websites, Forums and Chats, 2008-2009.

1. Description of the Sources, Qualification of the Authors and Contributors

Imamother.com
As the title may suggest (it is a pun: it can be understood as "I'm a mother" as well as "Ima – mother" - Ima means "mommy" in Hebrew), this site is especially devoted to women - actually, no man is even allowed on the forum. A minimal level of religiousness is even required to sign up, so it is a fairly narrow group. Logically, the average contributor is a married woman with children, but a wide variety of ages and social backgrounds are represented without a distinctive majority. With over five thousand members, it is by far the most important feminine Jewish forum on the internet. Its members are mostly American, and we can find a large sample of New Yorkese contributors.

Hashkafah.com
The title means "philosophy". This is probably the most famous Jewish American forum, and one of the oldest. Everyone is allowed in, so a wide variety of people contribute – even non-Jewish people interested in Judaism. The average contributor lives in New York area, is single, aged between 20 and 35 and fairly observant. University students and young

professionals are widely represented, so it is mostly an intellectual, so-called "high-class" public.

Askmoses.com

The primary goal of this site is to allow everyone to ask a question, in English, to a rabbi. Many different rabbis do answer the questions asked; all are Orthodox. It is not really a forum, although there can be a sort of dialogue between the seeker and the rabbi. The respondents are mainly married Orthodox males living in large American cities, primarily in New York. There are other sites like this one (for example, **Askarabbi.com**) but **Askmoses** has the largest database available.

Judaism 101/Jewfaq.org

Initially this site was intended as an introduction to Judaism, but with time, many readers have asked more and more questions to the author, so it became a "Jewish F.A.Q.". The author, Tracey Rich, is not a rabbi and is famous for his very open religious views, by frequenting Orthodox synagogues as well as conservative congregations. Yet, the opinions expressed on this site always reflect the strictly Orthodox point of view. This site is so well organised that everyone can find interesting answers to his interrogations. Non-Jews, Reformed Jews, as well as Orthodox rabbis use it.

Ortorah.org

This is the site of the Or Torah ("The light of the Torah") congregation in Skokie, Illinois. It provides a lot of information about Judaism to encourage Jewish education.

Aish.com

The organization Aish Hatorah ("The fire of the Torah") provides support for Jews willing to become observant. Founded in Israel, this organization now has moved most of its activities in the United States, especially in New York area.

2. Linguistic Analysis

a. The Vocabulary

On the part of the contributors, we find that Yiddish words are often added to the English lexicon, as it is the case in the following examples:

"Most times the doc will just say "oh, it's a virus" and I feel I don't need to *shlep* to the doc for him to tell me what I already know"[99]. "Shlep" means "to drag along". The Yiddish verb is used here instead of the English one because of the familiar, informal connotation of the Yiddish verb "shleppen".

In most cases, Yiddish terms will be used as their equivalent does not seem to exist as such in English. These terms are cultural borrowings from Yiddish, and they will be used to avoid a periphrasis:

"Congratulations Shalhevet - you are a *yenta*!!!"[100] A "yenta" is a chatterbox. The Yiddish notion is retained as it is also intended to show a cultural proximity between the author and the recipient.

---

[99] On Imamother forum, user S, a 21-year-old chassidic ultra-Orthodox Ashkenazic woman from Ohio, married, with 2 children. Occupation: preschool teacher

[100] On Imamother forum, user G, a chassidic ultra-Orthodox Ashkenazic woman from New York, divorced, with 3 children, in her early 40's. Occupation: housewife

"When our couple and *einikel* come, then we are ten people"[101] "Einikel" is a grandchild. The difference between "einikel and "grandchild" is the affective nuance here conveyed by the Yiddish diminutive suffix –"el".

"Let a *shmock* just try that again!"[102] A "schmock" is a jerk. The Yiddish term is retained as it is very idiomatic and informal.

"September 27th seems to always be on *yontif*"[103] "Yontif" means "holiday, from Hebrew "yom tov"; the special meaning conveyed by using "yontef" instead of the English equivalent is that the author means to insist on the religious aspect of the holiday.

"[...] any potential *machateineste* will see through the thin veneer [...]"[104] "Machateineste" is used here as this family term simply does not exist in English: it means the other grandmother of one's grandchildren.

b. The Pedagogical Approach

On the part of the authors, we sometimes find a pedagogic approach as they try to teach the Yiddish word along with the translation and the religious explanation or answer a question. Examples can be seen on various websites:

---

[101] On Imamother, user D, a Litvish ultra-Orthodox woman from New York, married, with 6 children, in her mid 40's. Occupation: housewife

[102] On Hashkafah, user G, a modern Orthodox Ashkenazic man from New York, single, in his late 20's. Occupation: executive

[103] On Imamother, user A, a Yeshivish ultra-Orthodox woman from Illinois, married, with 3 children, in her mid 30's. Occupation: teacher.

[104] On Hashkafah, user J, An Orthodox Ashkenazic woman from New York, married, in her early 20's. Occupation: student

(Jewfaq.org) "Dreidel: A top-like toy used to play a traditional Chanukkah game."

"[The circumcision] is commonly referred to as a bris (covenant)".

In the Jewish sense of the term, a priest (kohein) is a descendant of Aaron, charged with [sic] performing various rites in the Temple in connection with religious rituals and sacrifices".

"A chazzan (cantor) is the person who leads the congregation in prayer".

"You may find a menorah (candelabrum) in many synagogues".

"Traditional Jews believe that The Temple will be rebuilt when the Moshiach (Messiah) comes".

(AskMoses) "Do I need a Get (Jewish Divorce) from my non-Jewish husband?"

(Torah.org)[105] "It may prove difficult to verify the lineage (yichus) of the child".

"Yichud (being alone), hugging, kissing, etc., are not permitted".

"The selected material covers the 613 commandments (*mitzvos*) of the Torah".

(Aish.Com) "Sadly, many have left Judaism and Jewish practice. This is a *shanda* [a disgrace]".

These reformulations attest of a will to retain the Yiddish terms along with their religious or cultural meaning to the

---

[105] This website "promotes further Jewish education about our Jewish roots, as represented in Jewish source".

effect of reconnecting the non-observant Jews to their culture via the traditional language of the Ashkenazic Jews.

c. The Fields of Vocabulary which are Most Impacted

As the classified recapitulative list of the found Yiddish terms shows, some topics are dominant. Unsurprisingly, the domains most impacted are:

Religious concepts, rituals and objects:

"Chazzan" (cantor), "kohein" (priest), "bris" (circumcision), "dreidel" (a traditional toy) "yontef" or "yontif" (holiday), "menorah" (candelabrum), "Moshiach" (Messiah), "get" (divorce), "yichud" (being alone), "mitzvah" (commandment), "yeshiva" (a talmudic academy), "hashkafah" (philosophy), "matir" (religiously allowed), (forbidden), "matsah" (unleavened bread), "halachic" (following the halakha, the religious laws), "chassid" (a type of strict Orthodox Jew), "baalas teshuva" (a female returnee to Jewish observance), "chochomim" (wise men), "shul" (synagogue)

Family Life:

"Einikel" (grandchild), "machateineste" (the other grandmother of one's grandchildren), "boychik" (little boy), "yichus" (lineage), "bris" (circumcision), "get" (divorce)

Human types:

"Yente" (chatterbox), "shmock" (jerk), "midda" (a personality trait)

Food and Cooking:

"Bagel" (a kind of bread), "kneidel" (matzah balls), "tschulent" (a holiday food)

<u>Greetings:</u>
"Gut yontef" (good holiday),"l'chaim" (to life)
<u>Feelings:</u>
"Shanda" (disgrace)

Thus we can see that most of the Yiddish vocabulary imported
into American English pertains to lexical fields that matter a
lot in the Jewish culture: religious objects and rites, family
ties, human characterizations, food, cooking. These topics are
all linked together (as we can notice the categories often
overlap), and constitute the back-drop of Jewish daily life.

While this added lexicon does not affect the structure of the
English language it does attest nevertheless to a degree of
coexistence, since American English (as Yiddish) "welcomes"
the loans and embeds them in its structure, as it does with
many other languages. This common point between the two
languages makes it even easier for them to melt.

d. Morphological Features

We will now analyze contexts where the mixing affects the
structure of the word. The linguistic phenomena prove rich
and diverse as a wide range of morphological Yiddish features
is to be found on the websites, forums and chats.

What is striking here is the manifested diversity as we find the
following range of morphological phenomena:

Plural Marks, Feminine/Masculine Marks :

"Do you use soft *matzos* on *pessach* ?[106] "Matsos" is the plural of "matsa" (the unleavened bread eaten on Passover - "Pessach"). Here the plural form is taken from Hebrew ("-ot"), so the final –s is not the English plural but the Yiddish "-os" transcription of the Hebrew letters "-ot", "vav" and "tav", the feminine plural mark.

"It's also a good idea to familiarize yourself with the stories of the *chochomim*."[107] "Chochomim" is the plural of "chochom", which means "wise man" (from Hebrew "khakham", same meaning). The Yiddish noun "chochomim" comes from Hebrew "khakhamim", and keeps its original Hebrew plural with a masculine –im ending .

"Do you have links to *yeshivish* schools and *shule*?"[108] This example provides us with an English suffix –ish added to the Yiddish word: "*yeshiva*" (a religious school where boys study the Torah). "*Yeshivish*" is meant to designate a category of ultra-Orthodox Jews whose main occupation is to study Torah. "Shule" is the plural of "shul", the Yiddish word used to designate a synagogue. The plural mark –e is the Yiddish plural.

"Someone who is a *baalas teshuva* gets their past erased..."[109] English nouns usually don't have a feminine form, but Yiddish

---

[106]   On Imamother forum, user S, a 21 year old chassidic ultra-Orthodox Ashkenazic woman from Ohio, married, with 2 children. Occupation: preschool teacher
[107] On Askmoses, Rabbi Tzvi Freeman, a Lubavitch ultra-Orthodox Ashkenazic scholar from New York
[108] On Imamother forum, user M, a 44 year old chassidish ultra-Orthodox Ashkenazic woman from New York, married, 1 child. Occupation: housewife
[109] On Imamother forum, user S, a 21 year old chassidish ultra-Orthodox Ashkenazic woman from Ohio, married, with 2 children. Occupation: preschool teacher

ones almost always do. In this example, the Yiddish feminine form has been used. It allows us to know that the subject is a woman: indeed "Baalas teshuva" means a female returnee to Jewish observance (a man would be a "baal teshuva").

"So maybe work on your *middos* and don't be such a # to others!"[110] "Middos" is plural for "midda", which is a personality trait. If it is not specified that it is a bad midda, then it has a positive connotation. The plural mark –*s* is not the English one but is borrowed from Hebrew: it is the transcription of the letters "-ot", "vav" and "tav", the Hebrew final for feminine plural ("midda"/"middot").

In the two following examples, the same Yiddish word ("Chassid", a category of ultra-Orthodox Jews, singular "Chassid"), is used with distinctive features that allow us to make the following remark: when used by observant people (who usually know some Hebrew), the Yiddish words coming from a Hebrew root bear the Hebrew –*im* plural (for masculine nouns):

(On Jewfaq) "Some Orthodox Jews, especially *Chassidim*, wear a distinctive style of clothing", while non-observant or non-Jewish people (usually non-speaking Hebrew), would rather use the English plural form, as in this example: "In neighboring Crown Heights the Lubavitcher *Hasids* wrestle with a far more irreconcilable succession problem: The biggest faction refuses to anoint a successor to Rebbe

---

[110] On Hashkafah, user S, a 26 year old Orthodox Ashkenazic woman from New York, married, 1 child. occupation: veterinarian

Menachem Schneerson" (Michael Powell - Washington Post - Sunday, June 4, 2006[111]).

From these examples we see that Yiddish borrowings can use Yiddish suffixes as well as English ones, depending on the word, the context and the speaker. We can notice that in a mixed English/Yiddish expression, the more observant the people, the more Yiddish they will put in (here, Yiddish suffixes). On the contrary, the less observant, or less implicated in Jewish culture the people are, the more English suffixes they will put in[112].

Sometimes, Yiddish plural nouns are simply using a *–s* English plural suffix. Looking at the examples, we can therefore notice that the degree of religious commitment or proximity to religion does have an impact on the bloggers' choice of expression.

Among the various other morphological features to be found in the corpus are:

Yiddish Nouns Turned into American English Verbs:
"If a kid is bar <u>mitzvahed</u> [...]"[113] Here, the verb "*to bar mitzvah*" is created, meaning "having a bar mitzvah" (a

---

[111]   This example is extracted from the general press in order to show the difference between the English and the Yiddish ending for a same word.
[112] Yiddish has three common forms of plural marks: for the nouns coming from German, we usually find a *–e* or *-en* plural suffix, as in "bagel, bagele", "Yid, Yidn". Plural nouns coming from Hebrew bear a *–im* (masculine) or *–os* (feminine) suffix, as in "Chassid, Chassidim" and "mitzvah, mitsvos". Some nouns that are typically Yiddish (they may have a foreign root but have been strongly modified) bear a *–ach* suffix, as in "kneidel, kneidlach"

[113] On Hashkafah, user M, a modern Orthodox in his late 40s, married, with several children. Occupation: teacher

ceremony where 13 years old Jewish boys become adults according to Jewish law, and responsible of keeping the Jewish laws). The word is obviously not English, but the *–ed* ending is.

"No issue of koshering the dishes" [114]The word *kosher*, "fit for consumption", is turned into a verb by the English *–ing* ending. "Koshering" is "to make kosher".

Other morphological features are still to be found:

Yiddish Nouns Turned into American English Adjectives:
"Weird halachic ruling of the week"[115] This is the title of a blog entry: It comes from the noun "halacha", "Jewish law", with the added English suffix "*-ic*". It means, "pertaining to halacha".

Yiddish Nouns Turned into American English Adverbs:
"If a certain minhag is practiced by everyone in the city (a "minhag hamakom"), then one is Halachically obligated to follow this custom".[116] This is a further derivation of the previous example. The adverb "halachically" is derived from the noun "halacha", meaning "Jewish law" (through the adjective "halachic"), and *–ly*, the English suffix used to mark the adverb. This adverb means, "according to halacha".

American English Nouns with a Yiddish Prefix:
"Hospital - schmospital". This is the title of a blog entry[117] written by a non-Jewish woman from Michigan. Here the

---

[114] On Imamother, user P, a 24 year old Orthodox Sephardic woman from New York, married, with 7 children. Occupation: housewife

[115] http://bloghd.blogspot.com/2005/07/weird-halachic-ruling-of-week.html

[116] On Askmoses, Rabbi Naftali Silberberg, a Lubavitch ultra-Orthodox scholar from New York

[117] http://jodyferlaak.blogspot.com/2006/12/hospital-schmospital.html

deformation of the word with the adding of the Yiddish derogatory compound of consonants "*schm*" gives the word a strong pejorative consonance[118].

American English Nouns with a Yiddish Suffix:
"Gamzu, your boychik looks so cute with his haircut!"[119] The Yiddish affective/ diminutive suffix "-*chik*" is added to the American English word "boy". A "boychik" is a little boy.

Yiddish Verbs with American English Endings:
"When I was a young mother, I *shlepped* the kids everywhere"[120] Here the Yiddish verb is conjugated following the English grammar's use, with a –*ed* suffix at past.

"I am not aware of any rav that *matirs* this. I have heard of it being *matired* in the course of treatment"[121] To "Matir" means "to allow". This Yiddish verb, coming from Hebrew, is also conjugated following the English grammar's uses: a final -*s* at the third person, and –*ed* at past.

As we can see, the phenomena of mixing Yiddish features into English morphology are more than common on the websites, forums and chats; and rather strikingly, there are many different types of morphological features to be found. We also

---

[118]   See also the well-known joke: "Oedipus, schmoedipus! As long as he loves his mother!", also cited by Sol Steinmetz, *Yiddish and English. The story of Yiddish in America* (Tuscaloosa and London: The University of Alabama Press, second edition 2001) :65
[119] On Imamother, user Y, a Lubavitch ultra-Orthodox woman from New York, married, with 2 children, in her late 20s. Occupation: babysitter
[120] On Hashkafah forum, user L, an orthodox Ashkenazic woman from New York, married, with 3 children, in her early 40s. Occupation: dentist
[121] On Imamother forum, user C, an ultra-Orthodox Litvish/Yeshivish Ashkenazic woman from New York, married, with 8 children, in her early 40s. Occupation: labour and delivery nurse

have seen that all parts of the speech are being impacted by these Yiddish features (nouns, adjectives, verbs, adverbs). We do find a real diversity and profusion of Yiddish terms and phrases in this corpus, which proves far more "productive" than the corpus of the *Forward*'s articles; this seems to be a testimony to a certain resurgence of Yiddish into American English, partly due to the media itself (the internet tends to recreate communities united by identity, common interests etc.), and partly attributable to the young Jewish generation's increased interest into its own culture, familial tradition identity, and religion.

On the whole, the renewed presence of Yiddish features into American English does attest of Yiddish being for this public a dynamic second language, which forms a somewhat impressive background to the dominant English language, and brings about specific features which manifest themselves quite regularly in the discourse, giving the sense of a creative "grammatical expansion", a language in the moving, a far cry from the "frozen" Yiddish patterns displayed in the *Forward*'s articles.

e. Syntactic Features

Although less important in number, some syntactic phenomena are also to be found in this corpus.

Sometimes English constituents will be reversed as is done in Yiddish, to emphasize a part of the sentence (topicalization):

"Oy, brilliant he is not!"

"Already you're discouraged?"

In the first example, the emphasized constituent is the adjective "brilliant", qualifying the person being talked about, while in the second one, the emphasized word is an adverb, "already".

The phenomenon of topicalization can also be found in this horoscope: "Taurus: April 20th - May 20th". Is it vacation time yet? Wow, you just started school and already you're so busy!"[122]

Another syntactic feature to be found on the forums is the linguistic pattern called "calque" (meaning the direct / literal translation of an expression/ syntactic figure from one language to another- here from Yiddish to English), as in the following examples:

"Close the light" (instead of "Turn off the light"). The sentence is based here on a literal translation of Yiddish "Fermach di lisht".

As for the recurrent phrase: "not knowing *from*", it is based on Yiddish "nit vissen *fun*", which means "not knowing about", "not understanding":

"Who knew from Iran? Who knew from Iraq?"[123]

"Case closed, then: Proust's madeleine did not, does not, and never could have existed. To put it bluntly: Proust didn't know from madeleines"[124]

The impact of Yiddish's sentence structure on American English syntax, like the one on morphology, although to a lower extent, is present on the websites, forums and chats

[122] http://www.ytv.com/etc/horoscopes/
[123] http://www2.trincoll.edu/~mendele/vol10/vol10036.txt
[124] http://www.slate.com/id/2118443/

analyzed, most strikingly by comparison with its total absence in the other primary sources analyzed.

And so when American English comes to be more thoroughly mixed with Yiddish (as it is the case in this fourth corpus), apart from the relatively numerous lexical borrowings, we are able to find a very wide range of morphological Yiddish features, and also a measure of syntactic features adding themselves up into American English, so as to produce a modified American English.

Part Four: Yiddish in American English: Sociological Determiners and Diachronic Aspects of the Mixing

I. Diachronic Aspects of the Mixing

In the time span of sixty years, and following the results of our analysis, we discern a descending and then ascending pattern which we interpret this way:

In our first primary source, the shop signs, the ways are open to a diversity of options: melting Yiddish into English; or retaining some, or many Yiddish features, in one's expression; although the shop signs are scarce and brief, the linguistic phenomena are rich and diverse.

From there we find in the second source, but even more strikingly in the third primary source (the *Forward*'s articles), a descending pattern tending towards linguistic assimilation into American English. This assimilationist trend is striking at least as far as the audience of the *Forward* is concerned. Indeed, the newspaper goes to great lengths to try and keep at least *some* Yiddish-origin words, concepts, expressions, as the newspaper's readers are perceived as being totally ignorant of their parents' and grandparents' mother tongue. Moreover, the authors of the articles, themselves seemingly ill at ease with their linguistic heritage, display mostly repetitive Yiddish terms and frozen patterns. Any creativity is absent from this corpus.

Then, for a very different audience, and also owing to the fluency, creativity and community-oriented nature of the internet, we witness a dynamic re-ascending trend as the Jewish committed observant public finds a rebound towards its assumed identity; we witness here a sort of "linguistic expansion" manifested in the creativity displayed by the authors and contributors in their re-appropriation of their parents' and grandparents' linguistic heritage; the Yiddish lexicon is expanded; the Yiddish-based morphological features are rich and diverse; one can note linguistic innovations; this rebound manifests itself not only on diachronic bases but also from a synchronic point of view, the average writers and readers of the *Forward* being rather non-religious and politically left oriented [125].

Given the history and background of the *Forward* indeed, one can presume that the newspaper's reader is on average non-religious, and rather assimilated; this means that the issues of religious origins and roots will be, at best, a private matter to him, or a non-issue.

This is not the case with the attending public of the internet media as we are now going to discuss.

---

[125] The *Forward* was from start "a defender of trade unionism and moderate, democratic socialism [...] It fought for social justice [...] In 1990 the Forward Association, the newspaper's non-profit holding company [...] committed to covering the Jewish world with the same crusading journalistic spirit as Cahan's Jewish Daily Forward [...] Goldberg took the reins in July 2000. He [...] (returned) to the populist, progressive spirit that was the Forward's hallmark in its early years [...] the newspaper took another bold turn by appointing its first woman editor, Jane Eisner, in 2008, a respected reporter, foreign correspondent, editorial page editor and syndicated columnist [...]", see www.forward.com/about/history

II. Sociological Determiners

1. Sociological Explanatory Factors

From the various examples retrieved on the internet sites, forums and chats (the most recent corpus being the one where we have valid sociological indicators: sex, age, marital status, religion, "level" of religion, occupation …), we can deduct a certain amount of tendencies about the contributors.

First, almost all the contributors are Jews, and a wide majority of them are from Ashkenazic origin. This means that our results will be relevant and our conclusions applicable, only to this concerned subpopulation. All the people quoted were born in the United States or in an English-speaking country like Canada, so English is the mother tongue of all of them.[126].

We also notice that non-Jews start using some very well-known Yiddish expressions such as "hospital - schmospital", therefore showing that these forms are being integrated into mainstream American English.

Secondly, we can distinguish in this subpopulation two main age groups: over 40 (the speakers above 40 are, by a majority, housewives), and people under 30. The two age groups distinguish themselves in the following ways: the older people use mainly the lexical and syntactic forms of borrowings. The

---

[126] Non-Ashkenazic Jews being very few in America (and most of them are settled on the West Coast), logically, Sephardic Jews know less Yiddish and therefore use it less (but we can see some rare examples of Sephardic students with a perfect command of Yiddish as they join prestigious Ashkenazic Talmudic academies in New York)

vocabulary is mainly informal ("shlepp"), and related to family ("einikel") or to food/drinking ("l'chaim"). The Yiddish syntax can be seen as a passed on mistake and not a voluntary modification, as these contributors probably heard and retained syntactic patterns from their immigrated parents or grand-parents whose mother tongue was not English[127]. As for the younger group, it uses many morphological features, essentially because of their "funny" effect. Their vocabulary is also more impacted by religion. This can be explained by the strong religious revival that hit America the last 20 years. Many Jewish schools are created, where Yiddish religious vocabulary is widely taught.

Thirdly, the level of religious implication of a speaker does have an impact on the type of Yiddish borrowings he uses. We have already seen that in a mixed English and Yiddish expression with several possibilities, the choice of using more English or more Yiddish is directly related to religious commitment. This can be explained by the habit of talking more frequently to other Yiddish speakers, but the use of Yiddish words is also a barrier against assimilation. Orthodox Jews (whether they are Litvish, Hassidic or moderns) want to keep their identity as strong as possible and using one's ancestral language is a strong barrier to assimilation. Of course, they learn and know English in order to be *integrated* (but not *assimilated*) into the American society, and use it as a common language, but they certainly don't want to lose their traditional culture. So they try to use as much Yiddish words

---

[127] See the topicalization and inversion patterns.

as they can - even if there is a perfect English equivalent. Non-Religious, Conservative and Reform Jews are less hostile towards assimilation, and therefore we see that their websites use far less Yiddish expressions than the Orthodox ones. Their use of Yiddish is often limited to a strictly historical (talking about the past in Eastern Europe) or gastronomic purpose. Finally, we found that the other parameters analyzed (family status, occupation) did not seem to have an effect on the use of Yiddish.

2. The Contributors' own Point of View

Another way of clarifying the sociological determiners is to listen to the contributors themselves. There seem to be two major types of adaptative modes as far as Yiddish-origin features in American English are concerned.

Some people seem to be able to juggle with the levels of melting- and at the same time they provide a confirmation of the public concerned by the linguistic phenomena involved: "We chassidim use a lot of 'oi' [typical Yiddish ways of expressing yourself], but I certainly won't do it at work – also sounds silly when you're talking about sports or science!"

In this instance, the speaker adapts very intently and knowingly to the context by clearly differentiating between the public ("work") and the private sphere (family, or with other Chassidim) : he will not use Yiddish expressions or interjections in situations or speaking about themes that would not seem fit to do so.

Here we are clearly facing a "phenomenon of linguistic multi-system." Yiddish is only used when understanding is anticipated, and when the speaker deals with the topics that are the most impacted by Yiddish loans (religious issues and rites, family life, food …).

Indeed, as Chone Schmeruk puts it, there are "mutual relationships of the components of the polysystem"[128]:

These Jewish communities, in which people often used two or more languages, have been described by Ch. Shmeruk as a 'linguistic and cultural polysystem', in which various cultural components were 'engaged in a relationship or a dynamic of mutual influences'. In fact, these linguistic areas intermingled, overlapped and influenced each other, according to need, social situation or level of use. Even where a linguistic separation was strictly maintained, a certain porosity existed between the Jewish world and its cultural environment, whether German, Italian or Slav, and transfers occurred between scholarly and popular culture.[129]

Some other people seem to struggle more with the system; they may find it hard to switch ways of speaking, and will choose not to adapt when it is too difficult. Having specific Yiddish words available to avoid periphrases can also encourage them to use these words. It is certain that if Yiddish wasn't, to some level, or to some people, integrated in

---

[128]   Chone Shmeruk, "Hébreu, yiddish, polonais : une culture juive trilingue" in *Le yiddish: langue, culture, société* (Paris: CNRS Editions, 1999): 180

[129]

     http://poj.peetersleuven.be/content.php?url=article&id=504918&journal_code=SR

American English, it would be much more problematic not to adapt:

> I often have a hard time at work because I want to use a Yiddish word that doesn't easily translate into English. For example, once I was presenting my research at a department seminar and someone asked me about a point that was being debated in the scientific community. I said, "It's a machlokes." I could have said "There are competing schools of thought" but machlokes was so much easier. Fortunately, the person who asked the question understood, but most of the audience was perplexed.[130]

In this case, we see that the speaker did not adapt out of some routine ("machlokes was so much easier"); he then experiences difficulty ("most of the audience was perplexed"). We have here an example of a wrong decision in code-switching; at the same time, the speaker probably anticipated that at least *some* people would understand him, and this is why he did not adapt: he did not deem it indispensable.

Cultural differences can also cause people not to use only American English terms. For people familiar with Yiddish, "useful" terms enable them to easily express notions they are culturally used to. Later on, some of these words may be deemed useful by the non-Yiddish speakers, and thus be adopted into mainstream American English:

---

[130] On Imamother forum, anonymous user

Yiddish also developed a rich vocabulary of terms for the human condition, expressing our strengths and frailties, our hopes and fears and longings. Many of these terms have found their way into English, because there is no English word that can convey the depth and precision of meaning that the Yiddish word can. Yiddish is a language full of humor and irony, expressing subtle distinctions of human character that other cultures barely recognize let alone put into words.[131]

And so it may happen that American English (or more precisely here, New Yorkese English) will, in time, come to integrate Yiddish-origin words, morphological and syntactic features:

Yeah, it's definitely Yiddish, and so has become New Yorkese. (I love hearing recent immigrants from Asia and Africa using my grandmother's Yiddish constructions.) *Hey, schmuck! What gives? Move it already! Limo, schlimo. Smart, he isn't.*[132]

Also, some Yiddish terms will regularly be used instead of long periphrasis for the sake of "linguistic economy": the meat is "glatt kosher", in order to avoid going into details about how

[131]   Jewfaq.org
[132]   (On Metafilter, user CunningLinguist, a non-observant Jew from New York on its late 20's) : http://ask.metafilter.com/10341/

this is actually done[133]. It is the same thing with "cholov Yisroel"[134].

Last but not least, another explanatory factor, also put forward by the contributors themselves, throws further light on the subject of why people would voluntarily chose not to use English words:

> Christians say bad people go to hell and good people go to heaven, but most people need at least to go to purgatory first. Jews say bad people go to Gehinom and good people go to Gan Eden, but most people need at least to go to Sheol first.[135]

Here Yiddish words are being used in religious context, in a manner showing an "ideological" point of view, emphasizing the difference between Christianity and Judaism. And so the ethnic identity factor emerges as the most striking one in the renascence of Yiddish in American English.

---

[133] Kashrus (dietary laws) topics are complicated. "Glatt" kosher means that the meat is at the highest level of checking. Not only "kosher", but "extra" kosher. To make a meat glatt, the ritual slaughterer needs to check the animal extensively, and the process is quite complicated and precise. To avoid long explanations, people will just say it is "glatt kosher".

[134] "Cholov Yisroel", which translates as "milk of Israel", means that someone was there to make sure nothing non-kosher fell into the milk, from milking to buying. It is also ruled by precise and complicated rules.

[135] http://www.myjewishlearning.com/beliefs/Theology/Afterlife_and_Messiah/Life_Aft er_Death/Heaven_and_Hell.shtml

Conclusion

In this work we tried to analyze Yiddish-origin features in American English and at the beginning of this work, we put forward the following hypotheses:

-Yiddish, being *per se* a mixed language, would fairly easily mix with American English as it was the case when it consecutively encountered other cultures and languages in the course of history;

-As times goes, traces of Yiddish in American English would logically fade; nonetheless there could be backtrackings in this evolution, periods for which searching for one's roots would express itself by reconnecting to ancestral/ familial language, and thus leave traces on one's practice of American English; to that extent, we expected to find that the level of presence of Yiddish into American English would be linked to a speaker's level of religious practice, attachment to Jewish identity, and/ or link to a Jewish community.

The two hypotheses have been confirmed in this work.

The linguistic plasticity is retrieved, essentially in the fourth corpus as one witnesses the diversity of the morphological patterns regularly mixing English words with Yiddish suffixes. Interestingly enough, it is also the case in the first corpus, the earliest witness of Yiddish language encounter with American English; this is to say that we find this plasticity on the two ends of the chain as far as our research timeline is concerned.

Concerning our second hypothesis, although we did anticipate some sort of renewed link to Yiddish language and origins, we did not expect to find such a wide range of lexical and morphological Yiddish-origin features as displayed in the fourth period and source (that is to say, today and on the internet). These are to us witnesses to a new, uninhibited approach from the part of the immigrants' descendants: integration without assimilation; and, more than merely "remembering" one's roots, managing to make them present and alive in one of the most advanced outposts of today's Jewish life (after Israel): New Yorkese Yiddish English, on the internet.

Bibliography

Primary Sources

Printed Books

METZKER, Isaac. *A Bintel Brief: sixty years of letters from the Lower East Side to the Jewish Daily Forward*. Edited and with an Introduction by Isaac Metzker. Foreword and Notes by Harry Golden. New York: Schocken Books, 1971.

METZKER, Isaac. *A Bintel Brief Volume II. Letters to the Jewish Daily Forward, 1950-1980*. New York: The Viking Press, 1981.

The Forward's Articles

2003:

Lobbyist's New restaurants Put the 'K' in K Street, January 03, 2003, by Ori Nir

Orthodox Union Promises New Openness, January 03, 2003, by Alana Newhouse

Scholars Ask, What Would the Rav Do, January 03, 2003, by Alana Newhouse

Letter to the edition: *Who wears the Pants?* January 03, 2003

Recipe for Desunion, January 31, 2003

Only in America: Building Bridges at a Unique Seder, May 2, 2003, by Andrea Barron

The Stove's On – It Must Be Chicken in the Pot, May 2, 2003

Workmen's Circle Seder Hits High Note, May 02, 2003, by Masha Leon

Rabbi, Can You Spare a Dime? May 30, 2003, by Lisa Keys

Family Reunion at Home Plate, May 30, 2003, by Leonard Fein

Der Yiddish-Vinkl. A Weekly Briefing on the Mother Tongue, May 2 & 30, 2003

2004:

Uneasy Reading: Books About Parenting Fall Flat. The East Village Mamele, September 24, 2004, by Marjorie Ingall

2005:

Tango: Not Jewish, But Not 100% Not Jewish, June 10, 2005, by Alexander Gelfand

Confirmation: The Life And Times of a Modern Ritual, June 10, 2005, by Jenna Weissman Joselit

2006:

Remembering How the Yiddish Theater Turned Into Broadway, June 09, 2006, by Alexander Gelfand

2007:

The Bintel Brief. Dr. Ruth on *Beshert* Troubles, May 21, 2007

The Anti-'Fiddler, October 19, 2007, by Alexander Gelfand

2008:

2nd Ave Deli Cooks Up Controversy, February 22, 2008, by Gabriel Sanders

Hasidic Rabbi by Day, Pop Artist by Night, February 22, 2008, by Sara Trappler Spielman

High Cost of Living Leads Orthodox To Look Beyond Borders of New York, March 28, 2008, by Anthony Weiss

Songs of a Lost Tribe's Longing, September 12, 2008, by Joseph Leichman

Grandparents Circle in on Continuity, September 12, 2008, by Rebecca Spence

Chabon and Waldman: The Couple That Kvells Together, September 12, 2008, By Marissa Brostoff

2009:

The Bintel Brief. *Help! Our 6-Year-Old Son is More Observant Than we Are*, February 9, 2009, by Ayelet Waldman

The Bintel Brief. *How Do I Stop My Dad From Feeding Ham to My Kosher Son?* February 23, 2009, by Ayelet Waldman

The Bintel Brief. *Help! My Adult Daughter's a Schnorrer*, March 15, 2009 by J. Zaslow

A Prison Shul, Lost and Found, April 07, 2009, by Devra Ferst

Seder with the Obamas, April 24, 2009, Editorial

On the Jersey Waterfront, Jews Return, But Jewish Community Still Struggles, April 24, 2009, by Anthony Weiss

Websites

JewFaq: http://www.jewfaq.org
AskMoses: http://www.askmoses.com
FrumSpace: http://www.frumspace.com
Hashkafah: http://www.hashkafah.com
ImaMother: http://imamother.com
Chabad: http://www.chabad.org
Aish Hatorah: http://www.aish.com

Forums, Blogs and Chats

http://bloghd.blogspot.com/2005/07/weird-halachic-ruling-of-week.html
http://volokh.com/posts/chain_1102976665.shtml
http://www.caranddriver.com/columns/1897/tall-cars-are-coming-and-already-youre-liking-them.html
http://halachicinsights.blogspot.com/2009/04/more-pesach-insights.html
http://www.ytv.com/etc/horoscopes/
http://www2.trincoll.edu/~mendele/vol10/vol10036.txt
http://www.slate.com/id/2118443/
http://www.socialaffairsunit.org.uk/blog/archives/001566.php
http://poj.peetersleuven.be/content.php?url=article&id=5049
18&journal_code=SR

Secondary Sources

Printed Books

AUSUBEL, Nathan. *Pictorial History of the Jewish People.* New York: Crown Publishers Inc., 1953, 11th edition 1963.

BAUMGARTEN Jean, Ertel Rachel, et al. *Mille ans de cultures ashkénazes.* Paris : Liana Lévi, 1994.

BLUESTEIN, Gene. *Anglish/ Yinglish. Yiddish in American Life and Literature.* Lincoln: University of Nebraska Press, second edition 1998.

CHOURAQUI, André. *Histoire du judaïsme.* Paris : P.U.F., 1968.

DOUBNOV, Simon. *Précis d'histoire juive.* Paris : Service technique pour l'éducation, 1ère édition 1933, nouvelle édition complétée 1963.

ERTEL, Rachel. *Le Shtetl. La bourgade juive de Pologne.* Paris : Payot, collection Le regard de l'Histoire, 1982.

FISCHER, Dominique. *Le Moïse des Amériques.* Paris: Grasset, 2002.

FISHMAN Joshua A. *The sociology of Yiddish.* In BAUMGARTEN Jean, ERTEL Rachel, et al. *Mille ans de cultures ashkénazes.* Paris: Liana Lévi, 1994.

FLEXNER Stuart Berg, *Preface to the supplement, Dictionary of American Slang,* (New York: Thomas Y. Crowell, 1960, supplemented ed., 1967).

Glückel. *The Memoirs of Glückel of Hameln.* New York Schocken Books, 1989.

HADAS-LEBEL, Mireille. Histoire de la langue hébraïque des origines à l'époque de la Mishna. Paris: Publications Orientalistes de France, 1977.

HARKAVY, Alexander. *Yiddish-English-Hebrew Dictionary.* New York : Hebrew Publishing Company, 1928.

JACOBS, Neil G. *Yiddish: A Linguistic Introduction* Cambridge: Cambridge University Press, 2005.

KATZ, Molly. *Jewish as a second language.* New York Workman Publishing Company, 1991.

KATZ, Jacob. *Exclusion et tolérance. Chrétiens et Juifs du Moyen-Age à l'ère des Lumières.* Paris: Lieu commun/Histoire, 1987.

KRIWACZEK, Paul. *Yiddish Civilization: the rise and fall of a forgotten nation.* New York: Vintage Books, 2005.

LEVENSTON, Edward A., Sivan Reuben. *The Megiddo Modern Dictionary English-Hebrew.* Tel Aviv: Megiddo Publishing Co. Ltd,

LEVITT, Corinne. *Les Juifs de New York à l'aube du XXIème siècle: communauté juive ou identités juives?* Paris Connaissances et Savoirs, 2006.

MENCKEN, H. L. *The American Language.* New York Alfred A. Knopf, 4th ed., 1936.

MUGGAMIN, Howard. *The Jewish Americans.* New York-Philadelphia: Chelsea House Publishers, 2001.

PATAI, Raphaël. *Tents of Jacob: the Diaspora – Yesterday and Today.* New Jersey: Prentice-Hall.

Pirké Aboth. Traité des principes ou recueil de préceptes et de sentences des pères de la synagogue. Paris: librairie Durlacher, 1957.

PRINCE, Ellen F. *Yiddish as a Contact Language,* in *Creolization and Contact,* Creole Language Library Volume 23, edited by Norval Smith and TONJES Veenstra. University of Amsterdam-Free University Berlin, 2001.

ROSTEN, Leo. *The Joys of Yiddish.* New York: Pocket Book Edition, 1970.

ROTH, Cecil. *The Jewish Contribution to Civilization.* Oxford: The East and west Library, 1945.

RUPPIN, Arthur. *The Jews of To-Day.* London: G. Bell and Sons, 1913. Pp. 310.

SANDERS, Ronald. The Lower East Side. A Guide to its Jewish Past in 99 New Photographs. New York: Dover Publications, Inc.: 1979.

SHEINMAN, Mort. *A Tenement Story.* New York: The Lower East Side Tenement Museum, 1999.

SHMERUK, Chone. *"Hébreu, yiddish, polonais : une culture juive trilingue"* in *Le yiddish: langue, culture, société.* Paris: CNRS Editions, 1999.

SMILEVITH, Eric, *Introduction aux Commentaires du traité des Pères (Pirké Avot)*, Lagrasse: Editions Verdier, 1990).

STEINMETZ, Sol. *Yiddish and English. The story of Yiddish in America.* Tuscaloosa and London: The University of Alabama Press, second edition 2001.

STRONG, James. *Hebrew Dictionary. A Concise Dictionary of the words in the Hebrew Bible, with their renderings in the authorized English version.* Madison, NJ, 1890.

TURNIANSKY, Chava. *Les langues juives dans le monde ashkénaze traditionnel*, in Baumgarten Jean, Ertel Rachel, et al. : *Mille ans de cultures ashkénazes*. Paris: Liana Lévi, 1994: TURNIANSKY, Chava. *Glikl : Memories 1691-1719*. Jerusalem: The Hebrew University of Jerusalem, 2006.

WEINREICH, Max. *History of the Yiddish Language*. Originally published in 1973 in Yiddish by the YIVO Institute for Jewish Research. With Paul Glasser, Shlomo Noble (translation): *History of the Yiddish Language* (London- New Haven: Yale University Press, Yale Language Series, 2008).

WEINREICH, Uriel. *Modern English-Yiddish, Yiddish-English Dictionary*. New York: YIVO institute for Jewish Research – McGraw-Hill Book Company, 1968.

WEX, Michael. *Kvetch! Le Yiddish ou l'art de se plaindre*. Paris: Denoël, 2008.

YADIN, Ygael. *Bar-Kokhba, The rediscovery of the legendary hero of the last Jewish revolt against Imperial Rome*. London – Jerusalem : Weidenfeld & Nicholson and Steimatsky, 1971.

YADIN, Ygael. *Masada, la dernière citadelle d'Israël*. Paris : Hachette, 1966.

Printed Periodicals

GANS, H.J. "The 'Yinglish' music of Mickey Katz", *American Quarterly* 21, 1953

BARNHART, Clarence L. "On Matters Lexicographical", *American Speach* 45, 1973

KABAKCHI, V.V. and DOYLE, C.C. "Of sputniks, beatniks and nogoodniks." *American Speech*, Vol. 65, No 3, Autumn, 1990

BECKERMAN, Gal. "Forward Thinking. So what if the Goyim are looking? A Jewish Newspaper lets it all hang out", Columbia University, Graduate School of Journalism, *Columbia Journalism Review,* Volume 42, Issue 5 (January 2004)

Articles on the Internet

SIEGEL, Jennifer. "A Community of Readers", *The Forward,* (Issue April 6, 2007), http://www.forward.com/articles/10463/ (accessed October 2009)

Persée, Portail de revues en sciences humaines et sociales. http://www.persee.fr/web/revues/home/prescript/article/rfsoc_0035-2969_1985_num_26_2_3948: « Wette, wedding. Un texte inconnu de Mauss », in Revue française de sociologie année 1985, Volume 26, n° 26-2

PRINCE, Ellen "Yiddish as a Contact Language", The Pennsylvania State University (November 1998), http://209.85.229.132/search?q=cache:SJCWix7qKzcJ:ftp://babel.ling.upenn.edu/papers/faculty/ellen_prince/creole.ps+Yi

ddish+as+a+Contact+Language+University+of+Pennsylvani
a&cd=2&hl=fr&ct=clnk&gl=fr (accessed October 2009)
KALSON, Sally. "Yiddish survey aims to find how
Americans use Jewish-influenced words ", Pittsburgh Post-
Gazette (Issue August 19, 2008), http://www.post-
gazette.com/pg/08232/905240-51.stm (accessed October
2009)

Consulted Websites

American history and world history:
http://www.historycentral.com
The American Jewish Joint Distribution Committee:
http://www.jdc.org/jdc-history/years/1914.aspx
The Jewish Encyclopedia:
http://www.jewishencyclopedia.com
The Jewish Language Research Website, produced and
edited by Sarah Bunin Benor, Hebrew Union College:
http://www.jewish-languages.org
The Immigrant Heritage Trail Web site, a project of the Lower
East   Side   Tenement   Museum:
http://www.immigrantheritagetrail.org/?q=node/401
The New York City Museum:
http://www.mcny.org/museum-collections/painting-new-
york/pttcat109.htm
TorahsPlus Judaica. http://www.torahsplus.com/about.asp
Concordance Strong Français. Lexique de l'ancien testament
hébreu (et araméen) :
http://www.strong.kabbale.be/strong_hebreu/strong-hebreu-
7008.html

"THE GIVEN NAMES DATA BASES" (GNDBs) Professor
G. L. Esterson, Ra'anana, Israel.
http://www.jewishgen.org/databases/GivenNames/

Glossary of Yiddish Terms

Baal teshuva: returnee to Jewish observance.

Bagel: Small ring-shaped bread

Beshert: Soulmate

Bris: see bris milah

Bris milah: Circumcision. It is seen as the symbol of the covenant between God and the Jews, and probably the most well-known and observed mitzvah.

Bubbe: Grandma

Chassid: Person belonging to a chassidus.

Chassidic: Pertaining to chassidus.

Chassidus: Community of Chassidic Jews led by a rebbe, or the Chassidic philosophy. The most famous communities are Chabad Lubavich, Breslov, Bobov and Satmar. Although they have the same Chassidic philosophy, they have their own customs, dress and culture, often influenced by their original country. These communities are part of the ultra-Orthodoxy.

Chassuna: Wedding.

Chochom: Wise man.

Chutzpah: insolence, nerve

Dreidel: A top-like toy used to play a traditional Chanukkah game.

Einikel: Grandchild.

Frum: Pious. Depending on the circles, it can mean someone keeping kosher and shabbes, or someone keeping a lot more things.

Gehinom: the Jewish hell. Contrary to the Christian one, it is only eternal for the monsters.

Get: Divorce according to halacha.

Haggadah: Book relating the escape from Egypt traditionally red on Passover

Halacha: Jewish law.

Kareit : Spiritual excision, it is the punishment for big transgressions and is only « curable » through teshuva or a time in Gehinom.

Kavod: Honor.

Kvatter: Person who brings the baby to the mohel. It is a kavod often given to the grandfather, and also a segula to have children given to infertile couples. Colloquially called Godfather.

Lechaim! : "To life!" It has customary for Jews to say this before drinking wine since the early Middle-Ages.

Mamzer: Bastard

Matsa: Flat unleavened bread that observant Jewish people eat during Pessach instead of bread.

Mazel tov: "Good destiny!". It is said when you hear of a good event. A common mistake is to use it like "good luck", when someone needs to encouraged.

Mentsch: A [great] man.

Mitzvah: Means "law" and "good deed" at the same time. You have to do it, but you still get rewarded.

Mohel: Circumciser. He must be an observant Jew who followed a very long and serious training. Nowadays, he is often a doctor too.

Moshiach: Messiah.

Nebech: A poor guy, a "case", or a person who suffers because he makes other people's problems his own.

Pessach: Hebrew for Passover, this holiday commemorates the liberation of the Hebrews from slavery in Egypt. Pessach means "passing over/skipping".

Pupik: Navel

Rebbe: Leader of a chassidic community. Often hereditary.

Schmalz: Chicken's fat

Schmock: A jerk.

Segula: Treasure, or amulet.

Shalom: The traditional Jewish greeting. It means "peace", but also gives an idea of wishing wholeness and even perfection to the greeted person.

Shidduch: Match met or introduced to someone wanting to get married.

Shikkur: Drunk

Shlemiel: A person who suffers due to his own poor choices or actions, or more simply a moron.

Shlep/Shlepping/Shleppen: To drag along.

Shlimazl: A person who suffers through no fault of his own, who is always unlucky.

Shul: Synagogue

Talmud: Rabbinical development and explanations of the Torah.

Tatte: Dad.

Teshuva: Repentance.

Torah: The Old Testament, the "Jewish Bible".

Tukhes: Bottom (familiar)

Yeshiva: School where boys learn the Torah and the Talmud.

Yeshivish: Non Chassidic ultra-Orthodox Jew, or pertaining o this category.

Yichus: Pedigree, family background. It is both an advantage (the merit of the ancestors is said to influence the descendants positively) and a responsibility (you have to be worthy of your ancestors).

Zayde: Grandpa

Made in the USA
Coppell, TX
13 August 2023

20322780R00090